A SWEET
FLORAL LIFE

A SWEET
FLORAL LIFE

Romantic Arrangements
for Fresh and Sugar Flowers

Natasja Sadi

with Sarah Owens

TEN SPEED PRESS

California | New York

Voor Jan en Nora

Contents

INTRODUCTION
A Passion for Flowers 1

PART I
No Present Without the Past

CHAPTER ONE: Redefining the Golden Age 17

PART II
At Home

CHAPTER TWO: Delftware 47
CHAPTER THREE: Flowers for Living and Entertaining 57

PART III
Creativity

CHAPTER FOUR: Nurturing Intimacy with Nature 71
CHAPTER FIVE: The Art of Arranging 77
CHAPTER SIX: Photography 89

PART IV
The Arrangements

CHAPTER SEVEN: Searching for Flower Gold 107
CHAPTER EIGHT: Fresh and Sugar-Sweet Seasonal
Arrangement Guides 133

PART V
Sweet Moments

CHAPTER NINE: Creating a Sweet Garden 183
CHAPTER TEN: Celebration Cake 229

Resources and Bibliography 238
Acknowledgments 241
Index 242

A Passion for Flowers

To live in Amsterdam is to be surrounded by history and flowers. From the iconic seventeenth-century canals to the houses that line them, the past lingers on architectural facades and further below, submerged in the wooden beams that hold this city only slightly above water. Each day, I wake to the chime of the Westerkerk bell tower, which has been ringing since the early 1600s. Its daily companionship is a call to remain present in the sounds, smells, beauty, and trade that created and continues to embody the identity of my charming city. As I mount my bicycle to visit the Saturday morning flower market, I anticipate filling my basket with the last of the Netherlands' famous tulips, frilly ranunculus, and maybe a few early peonies if I am lucky. These glorious blossoms are only a few among the many choices of locally grown flowers that are my country's point of pride. I arrive early and without expectations, ready to let the colors, textures, and forms on display call to me as I visit with my favorite vendors.

My selections barely fit into my bicycle's basket, and I must mind the cobblestone bumps as I journey back home to my atelier. Depending upon my projects, some weeks I require two trips: the first batch of flowers hastily deposited into the foyer while I return to the market to collect the remaining bundles necessary for my tasks.

Once home, I climb the narrow steps of our eighteenth-century merchant house to the upper floor and emerge onto the roof that towers over the gates of the city. Up here with the full scope of Amsterdam's canals in view, I observe the pots in my rooftop garden that overflow with seasonal plants developed at the hands of multigenerational Dutch farmers. I pluck a few blossoms and bring them back to the sink, admiring how their wild and windblown character mingles with their highly cultivated cousins.

I settle into an afternoon of quiet solitude with a warm cup of tea by my side, and the fun begins with arranging the blossoms into a cheerful riot of color. Each Saturday's bounty inspires a week of seasonal celebration as I place the flowers into delftware vases. These arrangements fill my family's home with warmth as they settle into bright corners or ramble across the dinner table.

This passion for living with flowers developed over time into a multifaceted livelihood. As more people all over the world desire permanent images of these compelling creations in their homes, my photography of my arrangements has evolved to capture them in the moody northern light for limited-edition prints. I must wait for just the right moment of light before capturing their ephemeral beauty with my camera. During this time, I notice how the flowers relax and open, changing their relationship in the vase. If there is anything more satisfying than composing an arrangement, it is seeing it displayed on the wall of a beautiful home, ten times its original size and coated in high-gloss resin!

I step back and admire my sumptuous floral bounty before more closely considering its details. What comes next is a long stretch of time studying, sculpting, and painting the individual parts of each flower in sugar paste, an edible medium that pleasantly brings out the perfectionist in me. I owe this in part to the generous inspiration and resources that Amsterdam provides to study the infinitely varying forms, colors, and textures of seasonal flowers. The accessibility of so much abundance is endlessly inspiring. Because my sugar flowers look so real, they are often mistaken for their perishable counterparts and are especially suited for decorating lavish celebration cakes (see page 229), which are in popular demand for their keepsake qualities. Each day is a race against time to record the glorious moments of the flowers that change with every hour.

This work culminates in a triumphant manifestation of nature's splendor, and as I reflect on another week passing, I can't help but become nostalgic. The many threads that have woven my life together as an artist are all present and laid before me in a full-circle moment.

I never would have anticipated living this flower-filled life, but what a joy it is to spread so much love for natural beauty. Teaching these skills to others has taken me to the far reaches of the world, including Jakarta and South Africa, London, and New York, where I have discovered a common language with others who spend their days admiring and working with flowers.

The joy and wonderment of nature has built a bridge between my past and present moments of pleasure.

Beginnings

Exploring creative expression began when I was very young. My mother and I emigrated from our South American home country of Suriname to the Netherlands when I was only four years old. Seeking new opportunities, my mother worked hard to establish herself and provide for our family at the sacrifice of our time together. As I grew older, I spent hours entertaining myself with design projects, mostly hidden from view to avoid being reprimanded. I stitched together anything I could get my hands on and fantasized about working with opulent fabrics and lace. Despite my obsessive desire to become a skilled fashion designer, my habits were not encouraged, especially when my mother discovered I'd sacrificed her precious linen collection to make fanciful pillows. As I grew older, creating gorgeous dresses became an important refuge from the expectations of the practical studies and affluence that were imposed upon me, like so many other first-generation emigrants. This passion allowed me not only to dream but to bring my visions into reality at the will of my own hands.

When it came time to choose a subject to study, I followed my heart and pursued a career in fashion design. This decision was not popular with my family, who believed that I should follow a more prescribed path to success and happiness. Within my family's circle, there were few examples of successful creatives who shared our history or looked like me. Like many immigrant children, I felt pressure to become a doctor or lawyer to not only please my parents but also to prove my value to Dutch society, especially as a brown-skinned woman of mixed heritage. It would have been easy to let this conditioning steer me away from what my heart truly wanted, but despite my family's understandable resistance, I forged ahead.

My aspirations and determined nature were eventually rewarded with loyal clients from fashionable cities of Europe, such as London, Geneva, and Paris, and further abroad all the way to Asia. These clients appreciated my ability to sculpt with fabric and dress them with unique statement pieces for lavish weddings, parties, and press events. For nearly twenty years, I honed my fashion design skills and thrived in creating a romantic ambiance for my international clients. I loved decorating my studio with elaborate flower arrangements, which my clients came to anticipate during their fittings. The forms and textures of the blossoms provided festive inspiration for our meetings and complemented the style of my designs. Whenever the opportunity presented itself to use silk flowers as dress adornments, I would become giddy with excitement. Elaborate embellishing roses made from sparkling beads or a veil embroidered with the arching stems of the delicate lily of the valley would make my heart skip a beat!

It wasn't until after the birth of my own daughter that I took a step back and reconsidered my relationship to my process. I did not know exactly how my work needed to evolve, but I knew it needed a renewed sense of purpose and connection to what inspired me. What happened next is an unexpected twist of fate that resulted from a desire to give my daughter everything I had wished for at her age. While decorating a themed birthday cake for her, I discovered the malleability of sugar paste and fell in love with the possibilities of using it to sculpt realistic flowers. What followed was a deep exploration into not only delicious expressions of celebration, but the intimate relationship with nature that can develop when pursuing its imitation. As my interest grew in the production of sugar, I discovered its uncanny connections with my own family history. From plant breeders and flower farmers, to scientists, painters, and merchants of the Dutch Golden Age, a layered history unfolded before me, including the roles my ancestors played in the sugarcane fields of Suriname. I discovered my true calling to work in sugar, merging these all together in a contemporary interpretation of my ancestors' legacy.

Sugar Flowers

The question that I am asked most often is "What exactly are sugar flowers?" The answer is both simple and complicated: A little powdered sugar held together by egg white and a hardening agent creates a paste that is the base of endless sculpting possibilities. To model sugar flowers with accuracy requires studying the intricate relationship of the parts of the flowers, much as the naturalist and scientific illustrator Maria Sibylla Merian did in her groundbreaking drawings of the metamorphosis of insects in the 1600s (see page 27). Sugar paste allows each dusty stamen, blushing petal, and curve of the stem to be expressed with subtlety and grace. Sculpting with sugar paste is an elegant and sustainable technique that can both convey ephemerality and capture seasonal abundance in a permanent collection of flowers, to be enjoyed no matter the time of the year. Whether preserved under a glass dome, captured in a photograph, or adorning a cake, these flowers beg the eye to question reality. I never tire of requests from admirers to identify which flowers are not "authentic."

Creating sugar flowers has become deeply personal to me, beyond a lively connection to the senses. Although there are similar sculpting processes in clay, silk, and paper, I intentionally remain loyal to using sugar. This honors my African and Indonesian ancestors who worked in the sugarcane fields of Suriname, the Dutch colony where I am from, which gained its independence only in the year I was born. The enslavement of my ancestors and their hard labor were the price paid for extravagant foods such as sugar, initially enjoyed only by the wealthy. The sacrifices my ancestors made with their bodies, their spirits, and their lives laid the foundation for the middle class of seventeenth-century Europe to experience sweetness. Sculpting in sugar not only keeps the memory of these family members alive but also reframes the grim consequences of their fate and—for me—releases them from a painful narrative. This preserves their identity through an expression of splendor, each flower a joyful animation of their lives. Acknowledging this history can be difficult, but I hope that sharing my sugar flower techniques creates a new pathway to our collective liberation through beauty, creativity, and uninhibited personal expression.

Using This Book

This book is a collection of my self-taught processes of flower arranging, sugar sculpting, photography, and even some baking. I hope that it will deepen your own passion for flowers on a beautiful journey of creative purpose. It is a privilege to pass on what I have learned from the successes (and failures) that I've navigated over the years. When you use this book as a reference for inspiration, may it encourage you to let go of expectations and embrace the beginner's mind, even if you have some experience. It is with this freedom and fresh perspective that you will surprise yourself with new discoveries and expand your mastery of technique. The stories and techniques included in these pages reveal a deeply personal narrative and the particularities of what motivates my design aesthetic. I hope that what I share encourages you to seek and cultivate beauty in a way that feels just as personal and meaningful to you.

Each chapter not only brings your attention to subtle details but also has the potential to shift your thinking through awakening the senses. By providing a window into my reflections, I hope to open your eyes and heart to your own endless possibilities. With time and a little practice, you, too, will create a space of refuge where a passion for flowers can be cultivated. By learning from history and nurturing a gentle new path lined with petals, you have the potential to change your life for the better and create a future rich in endless beauty.

PART I

No Present Without the Past

To understand flowers in the modern Netherlands and how they have inspired my style, it is important to investigate the past to see how the unique appreciation for the floral arts developed. Living with flowers in the Netherlands has become commonplace, an inexpensive luxury that contradicts their once-feverish cultivation for the privileged few who could afford them. Market flower vendors are now abundant in the city of Amsterdam and throughout the Netherlands and are frequented by everyone. It is easy to find exceptional blossoms at affordable prices, making overflowing arrangements easier to compose than many would believe. Through hundreds of years of growing, breeding, and distributing, bulbs and cut flowers have become as synonymous with the Netherlands as the iconic windmills, wooden clogs, and cheese. The growers and breeders of the Netherlands have honed their expertise in creating the most exquisite blossoms in the world.

The obsession to possess and flaunt rare flowers began during the Dutch Golden Age (roughly 1575 to 1675), when Dutch naval expansion secured an empire of riches. This fertile time strengthened the Netherlands as a world power, and Dutch colonies were established on every continent with the labor of enslaved Africans and indentured servants recruited from Asia. These were my ancestors, the people whose lives and integrity I strive to honor and preserve with my sugar flower creations. Their sacrifice is often overshadowed by the opulence and grandiosity of this era, but it has shaped the floral artist that I have become. Just as a blank or negative space can emphasize the most subtle floral characters of an arrangement, the omission of important details in Dutch history only speaks to their significance. Despite (or perhaps because of) this shadowed legacy, the Netherlands has become a complex place of modern agricultural technology, great artistic expression, and cultural diversity.

...ding van Flora

...N DAVIDSZ DE HEEM EN ZIJN KRING

CHAPTER ONE

Redefining the Golden Age

It takes less than ten minutes to cycle from my home to the Rijksmuseum, one of the most beautiful museums in the world with priceless paintings, such as Rembrandt van Rijn's *The Night Watch* and Johannes Vermeer's *The Milkmaid*. While I ride past the beautiful facades of the canal houses, I imagine that some of these paintings once decorated their walls. These historic homes were built in the sixteenth, seventeenth, and eighteenth centuries and tell two stories: one of economic prosperity reflected in architectural beauty and the other of great hardship. The latter is difficult to address for many Dutch citizens, and history books often focus on the details of acquisition and discovery. But while the Dutch conquered lands and established colonies on all continents, they committed atrocities to inhabitants in the Americas, Asia, and Africa.

My enslaved and indentured great-grandparents helped build the wealth of this country but never dreamed that someday their great-granddaughter would live in the former canal home of a wealthy merchant, retelling their story from a different but equally important perspective. Reclaiming their narrative not only acknowledges the trauma of the past but allows me to move beyond its pain into a new and equitable creative footing. When shame and guilt are left behind, we can participate in and celebrate the beauty of collective healing.

An Age of Tolerance

The extravagance of the nouveau riche funded the expansion of the arts in Europe during the Age of European Expansion (roughly the fifteenth to eighteenth centuries), a loose term used to describe when seafaring Europeans began exploring already inhabited regions across the globe. Before the Golden Age, the Netherlands was occupied by the Spanish, and King Philip II reigned with a brutal hand. After winning the Eighty Years' War against the Spaniards in 1648, the Dutch regained political and religious independence. Many newcomers with great knowledge in the arts, crafts, and literature relocated to the Netherlands because of this newly inspired setting. As the Netherlands grew wealthier, the Dutch embraced diversity within population growth, and a unique style of creative expression emerged that persists even today. The appreciation of the contributions by craftspeople from all over the world has continued to shape a nation of great cultural diversity and artistic expression.

The Dutch Global Influence

At the end of the sixteenth century, the Netherlands was at the center of world trade, exchanging linens, silks, spices, and sugar. Amsterdam became the largest hub in the world that shipped, traded, and redistributed goods to the farthest stretches of naval exploration. In 1602, the Dutch East India Company (Vereenigde Oost-Indische Compagnie, or the VOC) was founded, followed by the West India Company (West-Indische Compagnie, or WIC) in 1621. Both exercised a monopoly in trade. The Dutch eventually gained control of the sugar industry with their South American colonies, and hard labor was imperative to make the sugarcane plantations profitable. Although the focus of the Dutch East India Company was on spices, silks, and porcelain, its West India counterpart dominated the sale and trade of slaves as personal property in North and South America.

Great strides in the processing of raw materials and the industrialization of agriculture, in addition to the exploitation of labor, maximized profits for both Dutch companies. Amsterdam became powerful, with an international influence that lasted for more than a century; money was pouring into the Dutch Republic for a select group of aristocracy, and the nouveau riche had money to spend. Beauty was for sale, and the arts, science, and literature greatly benefited from this prosperity. With Rembrandt, Vermeer, Frans Hals, and Rachel Ruysch, the Dutch Golden Age of the arts was born. It was also around this time that flowers became a must-have—the ultimate luxury good.

Scientific and botanical discovery also helped influence the use of natural resources that mirrored the spread of Western imperialism. Live exotic plants, detailed botanical illustrations, and stylish Dutch delftware vessels for sugar and precious flowers became symbols of affluence during this time. Stunning but fictitious still-life paintings of bouquets spilling with flowers from all seasons became a more accessible and permanent representation of fleeting beauty. Studying these important works increases our understanding for their context and offers clues to the modern artist for creating compelling compositions with light that directs our attention to detail and emotion. By recognizing the choices that were made during this time, we can develop a new and more honest appreciation for these remarkable arts and sciences. It is also an opportunity for healing and collective growth from a legacy of brutal manipulation for monetary gain and privilege.

Sunflowers and dill as companions to eighteenth-century waybills framed in the background. These relics describe the sea trade of the merchant who originally built and lived in our home.

The Legacy of Rachel Ruysch

If we are lucky, our parents provide for us an environment that nurtures our impressionable personality, encourages us to think critically, and fosters our emerging creative abilities. But imagine growing up in a home that is a literal museum, full of curiosities that your peers, let alone their parents, have never seen before or could even fathom existed. This was the early life of Rachel Ruysch (1664–1750), one of the most talented Dutch still-life painters and an artist who has continuously influenced my work.

Rachel's father, Frederik Ruysch, a professor, an influential botanist, and an anatomist, recognized the healing powers of plants for the human body. His insatiable curiosity about the spoils of global exploration resulted in one of the largest European collections of curiosities, a *Wunderkammer*. He was world famous for his scientific studies during a time when information and communication were sometimes oceans apart rather than an instantaneous digital click away. The Ruysches' home was filled with taxidermy animals, preserved body parts, and fetuses eerily floating in formaldehyde-filled glass bottles, displayed between rare plants from distant lands and insects proudly delivered to the Netherlands by boatsmen from the East and West Dutch India companies. The exoticism of these items drew the interest of influential academics and even royalty, including the czar of Russia. The Ruysches' home in Amsterdam must have been an incredible sight. How magical for a young child like Rachel Ruysch to grow up in an environment where science and wonderment were always center stage—a museum come to life!

Frederik encouraged Rachel and her sister Anna to observe and document nature, and they both began studying with accomplished painters at a very young age. They were incredibly talented floral and still-life painters who, working from their father's collection, depicted nature with remarkable detail and accuracy. Highly talented, Rachel was just fourteen years old when she started sharing her sketches and drawings with the public. While Anna stopped painting at the age of twenty-one, Rachel continued with professional dedication. She eventually married Juriaen Pool, a portrait painter, and together they bought a house on the Bloemgracht (flower canal) across from the Westerkerk church and a couple of streets from Rachel's family home.

Rachel Ruysch, Vaas met Bloemen
(Vase with Flowers)*, 1700. Mauritshuis Den Haag, the Netherlands.*

The depth and skill of Ruysch's renderings were considered by the public to be a testament to God's divinity and were much sought after by royalty and the nouveau riche. Her paintings were priced between 70 and 1,400 guilders, an extraordinary amount at the time, eclipsing even Rembrandt. The importance and popularity of her work are a great source of inspiration, especially considering the obstacles that women of her era faced in becoming successful artists. She bore ten children, but this did not stop her from producing the high-quality floral paintings that we still admire to this day. I have two children whom I love dearly, but I cannot imagine producing such prolific work of outstanding quality while balancing the demands of motherhood!

Ruysch combined flowers in her paintings that would not have otherwise been blooming in the same season and acknowledged that time can either nurture or terminate life. She had an eye for detail and depicted the truth of decay that must have been instilled by her father; she often included all stages of a flower's life in her paintings, from bud to fading bloom. These arrangements and their accompanying insects and fruit were full of symbolic meaning and hinted at luxury, subject to Dutch fashion of the time. Although flowers have a relatively short bloom time, painting them on canvas granted them the status of immortality, while insects like a caterpillar or a butterfly were a way of addressing death and rebirth.

By using sugar flowers in my arrangements, I can work as Ruysch did to traverse the seasons and feature flowers in their varied states of expression alongside abundant displays of fruit to create lush still-life scenes.

The depiction of exotic flowers was considered highly valuable, and these often carried the most prominent positions in her arrangements; a daisy or a buttercup rarely appeared in paintings. The colors of Ruysch's paintings are so rich set against dark backgrounds and her attention to detail so astute that you can almost smell the scent of her flowers! Although I adore the forms and admire the symbolism of common flowers and even some weeds as much as more exceptional specimens, I am endlessly inspired by Ruysch's manipulation of light and use of contrast to feature her favorite flowers by making their colors and forms stand out. I apply this lesson to my arrangements by creating a moody backdrop using fabric or the blackboard in my kitchen. When the natural light softens and I am ready to capture images, I adjust the composition in the frame or use reflective mirrors to emphasize the flowers that I deem worthy of interest.

Ruysch's painting *Vaas met Bloemen* (*Vase with Flowers*) is a prime example of how Ruysch conjured meaning in the realism of her work. It showcases a full arrangement of coveted flowers, from freshly harvested buds to rare blooms fading in exquisite ephemeral beauty. The most fascinating aspect, however, is a poppy stem cut with precise intention to remove the bloom. The absence of the bloom gives a feeling of emptiness to the otherwise abundant composition and makes the viewer question the importance of this dark, negative space. Does this truncated stem mean beauty is fleeting, or is it something more personal? Ruysch suffered heartbreak and loss when some of her children perished at a young age. Her floral paintings are an obvious documentation and appreciation of nature, but this spectrum of life and death speaks to a longing and grief that exists beyond a vase full of pretty flowers.

As summer transitions to autumn, peonies are missed, but their presence is immortalized through sugar, much as Rachel Ruysch painted flowers out of season. Both Ruysch's painted arrangement on page 21 and mine, opposite, use negative space to emphasize the relationships between its subjects.

New Amsterdam to New York

As expansion of European colonization continued, so too did the struggle for power and wealth. After many years of war between England and Holland, a Dutch fleet sailing with West India Company's sanction forced the British to capitulate when they seized Suriname (then a British colony) in the northeast corner of South America. The Peace of Breda was signed in 1667, awarding the British the Dutch colony of New Amsterdam, which they renamed New York, and English became the dominant language of the thirteen founding American colonies. In return, Holland gained Suriname from the British. Some Dutch people joke that it was a shame to relinquish New York, a bustling metropolis of wealth and fashion, for a rural South American jungle. Although it is questionable if the Dutch would have ever won the war with the British, I laugh at the thought of the modern world speaking Dutch, with its difficult-to-pronounce, throaty *G*! What the British gained in expansion into North America, the Dutch grew in wealth through the control of South American sugar production.

Time Capsules of Suriname

Slavery can seem like a distant tale in the Netherlands, something that occurred in faraway lands, separate from personal concern and the seemingly open-mindedness of modern Dutch society. The narrative of colonialism has been slow to shift since the abolishment of slavery, and because the lives of the enslaved were not well documented, their stories have largely been lost. It is estimated, however, that over the course of two hundred years, the Dutch enslaved more than 500,000 people to work in its colonies. About 30 percent of the enslaved people perished from disease and malnourishment en route to their destinations. It wasn't until 1814 that Holland signed an international treaty to end slavery, but it took until 1863 for the Dutch to enact the abolition of slavery. Even then, it was with great reluctance; the Dutch were one of the last nations to sign this historic treaty. After the abolishment of slavery, the few former slaves who did not flee were unwilling to do dangerous and difficult work, and the Dutch looked to the other side of the world for low-cost labor. Holland had already colonized the vast archipelago known as Nederlands-Indie (Indonesia) in 1816, but the presence of the Dutch East India Company had been established long before, in the 1600s. It is in this collection of islands where the Dutch found people willing to work in the fields of Suriname in return for the promise of great wealth. My maternal great-grandparents emigrated from Indonesia to Suriname during this time, and I am a descendant of both African slaves and Indonesian contract workers.

When I was fourteen years old, my mother and stepfather fulfilled my grandmother's dearest wish to visit central Java, and for the first time in her life, we traveled with her from Suriname, where she lived, to Indonesia via the Netherlands. She had only heard about this beloved country in tales described to her by her parents. We searched for Solo, the town my great-grandparents had left behind and which my grandmother had always remembered in their stories. We talked with people living there, searching for anyone who could provide us with information of our family. Many of the stories were passed down from generation to generation, but all of them were the same: a white Dutch person dressed like a rich man would recruit locals on the market square, telling them that if they boarded a ship, they would return wealthy. Desperate for a better life and perhaps some adventure, no one ever returned home after crossing the ocean. From one day to the next, people would disappear, never to be seen again. Frantic parents were left wondering what had happened to their children.

I have returned to Suriname several times with my mother later in life to revisit our homeland. On one unforgettable trip, we were in a remote, densely overgrown area when we stumbled upon two glass bottles half-buried in mucky-wet earth. As we walked through the bush filled with stately palm trees and exotic colorful fruits, we were lucky to come upon these artifacts, as they now mostly exist in museums. I did not know their significance, but my mother instantly remarked that they belonged to enslaved Africans or Indonesian contract workers who cultivated the fields. She explained that the water that filled the bottles was the only drink they would have to sustain themselves in the long days of backbreaking planting, weeding, and harvesting sugar or rice under a blistering tropical sun. It was a remarkable moment of reckoning, as we stood there swatting insects, our clothes drenched with sweat. This intimate encounter with the cruel reality of my ancestors made me realize how important it is that their story live on. The Indonesian side of my family is private about the details of the past, but I yearned to learn more about their lives before their grueling introduction to Suriname.

My mother was shaped by the hardship of our family in Suriname, and because of this, my childhood was not always easy. I have discovered that knowing and owning our narrative can break the cycle of transgenerational trauma and create a deeper understanding of its place in our lives. Accepting the inevitability and normality of ongoing pain is an important step in managing grief for lives lost or unwarranted cruelty. Rather than feeling bitter about what happened, survivors of enslavement, descendants of slave owners, or those who have experienced other forms of injustice can try to integrate it as a secondary experience rather than allowing it to continue to control their lives. This has been a lifelong process for me, and creating sugar flowers and floral arrangements in the Dutch style has been one way of processing history and breaking uncomfortable habits of silence. When we acknowledge but are no longer victims of suffering, it becomes easier to ensure a brighter and more beautiful future for our children, who can continue to bring about the change we want to see.

Suriname Through the Eyes of Maria Sibylla Merian

After three months crossing the rough Atlantic waters, Maria Sibylla Merian, her daughter Dorothea Maria, and an unidentified Amerindian woman who was their servant returned to Amsterdam from the Dutch colony of Suriname. Merian's research had been interrupted by illness, but this divorced mother of two had no regrets—her curiosity for the flora and fauna of this exotic and distant land must have outweighed her fears of the unknown. She had amassed many sketches, notes, and specimens that were almost too bizarre to be considered real, especially by other naturalists and artists like her. But as crates of lizard eggs and brandy-preserved snakes, hummingbirds, and caterpillars were unloaded, her celebrity status only increased, especially among her collectors. It was this undeniable proof combined with the artwork of her research that immortalized Suriname in the eye of eighteenth-century Europe and sealed Merian's reputation as one of the most important artists and scientists in history.

Born in Frankfurt, Germany, in 1647, Merian grew up during an era when women did not typically study art or science but were groomed instead to become mothers, govern the household, and take up polite hobbies such as embroidery. Like the celebrated painter Rachel Ruysch, Merian was fortunate to be surrounded by many working artists in her family. Her father, Matheus Merian, was a trained engraver and publisher who died when she was only three years old, and her mother remarried the celebrated floral painter Jacob Marrel, whose home studio focused on flowers and landscapes. From a very young age, Merian was exposed to books and journals of faraway places and viewed the world with the eye of an artist. Although her surroundings must have been tremendously encouraging, it was her curiosity and otherworldly talent that propelled her toward becoming one of the greatest botanical artists of all time.

From the age of thirteen, Merian was so mesmerized by the natural world that she began methodically studying insects with boundless dedication and patience. With her detailed, colorful botanical paintings, she not only identified and named new species of flowering plants, insects, and animals but also documented their

P. Sluyter Sculp

life cycles in ways that had never been done before. This was during a time when insects were thought to reproduce by spontaneous generation, almost as if by magic from piles of dung or rotting food. She quickly observed that there was so much more to learn and discover and was one of the first to document metamorphoses of the butterfly. Merian's work made a significant contribution to the fields of entomology—the study of insects—and ecology—the study of relationships among living things and their environments.

The elite's hunger for new and exotic findings meant that Merian's botanical illustrations were acquired by many influential collectors and royalty. Unlike Rachel Ruysch's paintings that defied the seasons and embraced fantastical combinations of lifelike flowers, Merian became famous for her scientific accuracy. Her clientele ranged from the Swiss court to Czar Peter the Great of Russia, a frequent visitor to Frederik Ruysch's *Wunderkammer* (see page 20), and one of Merian's many admirers. Despite her success, she longed to illustrate life beyond the dusty curio cabinets of dried specimens and their long-dead, faded insects. Merian was ready to embark on her own metamorphosis, a transformative experience on the shores of a faraway land.

At the time of her journey to Suriname, Merian was already an accomplished author, having published the two-volume work *Der Raupen wunderbare Verwandelung und sonderbare Blumen-Nahrung* (*The Caterpillars' Marvelous Transformation* and *Strange Floral Food*) in 1679 and 1683 as well as the three-volume *Blumenbuch* (*Book of Flowers*) in 1675–1680. But her last two years in Suriname were spent amassing those artifacts and drawings that would contribute to her life's work, *Metamorphosis Insectorum Surinamensium* (*The Metamorphosis of the Insects of Suriname*), published in 1705. This impressive tome beautifully illustrates the life cycle of one hundred insects and fifty-three plants and flowers.

Plate 45 in Merian's Metamorphosis Insectorum Surinamensium *is a watercolor of a peacock flower (*Caesalpinia pulcherrima*) with the life cycle of the Carolina sphinx moth (*Manduca sexta, *also known as the tobacco hornworm). In her text, Merian described how enslaved Africans used the flower to abort their children to prevent them from being born into a life of cruel servitude.*

The sheer volume of her work is not only masterful but overwhelming, an extraordinary achievement considering the extreme, unfamiliar conditions of this hot and humid land. It was a remarkable feat for a woman of her time, but her research, enabled by the knowledge and experience of the enslaved, remains relevant and inspiring, especially for those with a passion for flowers.

A seventeenth-century maritime journey from Amsterdam to Paramaribo, Suriname, could take months under bleak conditions; and because of hurricanes or pirate attacks, it wasn't uncommon for ships to never reach their destination. It was a bold decision in 1699 for a single mother to travel the dangerous waters with a twenty-one-year-old daughter in tow. But she was enabled by and benefited from connections to the Dutch sugar plantations that were already established in Suriname, helping to justify the voyage beyond her insatiable desire for discovery. I have traveled the dense interior jungle of Suriname with its stiflingly hot and humid climate and recall moments of shock running into a large, hairy spider or two. It was certainly courageous of Merian to take this journey and study the frighteningly large tarantulas and other alien insects, but the privilege of her class and her participation in colonial systems of slavery helped to seal her bravery in history.

Enslaved Africans and indigenous Arawak and Carib servants accompanied Merian and used axes to hack paths for her to walk, observe, and collect from the rainforest. She could not have documented the information in her book without the help of these slaves and servants, whose long-standing familiarity with Suriname contributed to her knowledge. They assisted her studies by bringing her caterpillars and providing additional information on the plants and insects she sought. Her Dutch companions thought her mad for giving attention to anything but sugar, which was deemed the most valuable commodity of the colony.

Indentured native women who helped Merian with housekeeping were particularly helpful to her understanding of plants and their use. Plate no. 45 of *The Metamorphosis of the Insects of Suriname* shares poignant information about the peacock flower (red bird of paradise) and the conditions under which the enslaved lived. "The Indians, who are not treated well when in service with the Dutch, use it to abort their children, not wanting their children to be slaves, like them. The black female slaves from Guinea and Angola have to be treated very kindly. Otherwise, they do not want children in their state of slavery and will not have any. Indeed, they sometimes even kill them because of the harsh treatment commonly inflicted on them, because they feel that they will be reborn in a free state in the country of their friends, as I heard from their own lips."

Two years after Merian's arrival at age fifty-two, her stay was cut short. The heat was simply too difficult to bear, and illness, likely mosquito-borne malaria, forced her return to Holland. She arrived home with her daughter and servant, whose knowledge helped her complete the descriptions of illustrations in her book. In the final years of her life in Amsterdam, Maria Sibylla Merian was a prestigious household name, and her work fetched handsome prices all over Europe.

When I travel abroad, people often ask me where I am from, but my appearance combined with the answer "The Netherlands" is confusing to many. When I explain that I was born in Suriname and raised in Holland, I am often met with even more puzzlement. My country of birth is not widely known, and now, sadly, Merian's name and her accomplishments are no longer the household topics that once put Suriname on the global map. Her story is, however, making a resurgence as more people with an interest in natural history and the floral arts discover her work.

Contemporary tales of Merian often sidestep her participation in slavery for her own benefit. Although this is troublesome, her work provides one of the earliest European accounts of seventeenth- and eighteenth-century Suriname, the country of my ancestors. When I am re-creating flowers in sugar, her detailed and accurate botanical drawings of pistils, stamens, stems, and sepals are invaluable company. The beauty of her drawings makes it easy to forget how she became such an important scientist, with groundbreaking discoveries that spanned over more than fifty years of research. By depicting insects together with rare plants and flowers, Merian gave us insight into the interactions of the ecological system. Through her descriptive writings, we also see into the lives of those who served her. This groundbreaking work continues to inform a new generation of scientific and creative discovery, but through a sharper lens of acknowledgment.

The Tulip: Lessons in Pursuit of Excellence

As much as I love the landscape and light of Holland, winter always seems excruciatingly long, especially to someone who hails from the tropics. After months of cold darkness, tulips are one of the first spring flowers to provide hope for warmer, brighter days ahead. They come in a riot of solid and sometimes striped (flamed) colors, from ivory to nearly black, and every pale and bright shade in between. Their elegant bell-shaped solitary flower is unique, and they are just as stunning tightly folded in bud as they are in full-blown open bloom. I can't think of a cultivated flower with more colors and forms than tulips, and their stems are always cheerfully dancing toward the light. They are also endearing drama queens that when left without water, droop despairingly but immediately resuscitate with just a sip of water; they are incredibly forgiving of neglect and can offer a lesson in resilience. When trimmed short, tulips can be charming bundled as a small posy, but when stems are kept long, they beg for attention and leave the viewer mesmerized. I am forever inspired by the multitude of expressions and gestures that they can convey in the vase or be captured in sugar.

No one flower symbolizes the Netherlands more than the tulip, and this association is based on one of the most fascinating botanical tales in history. An addition of a tulip, more than any other flower, creates that recognizable Dutch still-life feeling. Wild species of tulips originally inhabited the mountains of Central Asia, a recognized

biodiversity hot spot and the center of tulip diversity. It was introduced into cultivation in 1451 by the Ottoman Empire and, over the next century, found its way across Europe and into the hands of enthusiastic gardeners of nobility. These perennial bulbs flourished in our ideal weather conditions and *geestgrond* soils, a perfect combination of clay, loam, and sand. However, little was understood as to what influenced the appearance of tulips, and their mysterious but beguiling nature seemed to hold power over everyone who encountered them. Unpredictable tulip blooms transfixed the attention of the nouveau riche so much that wagers hinged on what impressive flowers would possibly emerge from their bulbs.

The flamed tulips, with dramatic stripes of color, were considered the most valuable, and their capricious nature became so tied to their superiority that speculation ran rampant and the famous "tulip mania" ensued. Regardless of economic standing, many people became flush with discretionary income from sea trade during this time, and clandestine tulip deals went down in dark, alcohol-filled cafés or on the newly formed stock market. The value of a single tulip bulb became so inflated that the Dutch economy eventually collapsed, bringing bankruptcy to many families. It is hard to believe that this historic economic crisis had what we now consider to be a common, albeit enthralling, flower at the root of the fallout.

We now know that viral infections are responsible for many tulip aberrations. What was once considered more valuable than a canal house is now every breeder's worst nightmare! Although tulips with stripes were all the rage of the seventeenth century and some are still celebrated, bulbs infected with unwelcome viruses are now destroyed immediately upon identification to avoid ruining others.

The Dutch are tradesmen at heart, and thankfully, some did not give up after the devastating economic crash caused by tulip mania. The modern Dutch floriculture industry is thriving, thanks to the foundations of discovery and lessons learned so long ago combined with innovative greenhouse and harvesting technology. Our small country currently supports almost eight thousand growers who cultivate thirty thousand different plant varieties. Each day of every season, millions of stems and plants are traded. Most Dutch citizens are keenly aware of our flower power, but this magnitude became visible to the rest of world at the beginning of the Covid-19 pandemic. When borders closed, millions of stems destined for markets abroad became tragic victims of shredders and trash bins.

Visiting a Dutch tulip nursery dedicated to cultivar development provides an intimate look into the life's work of a breeder. This floral oasis at the height of spring appears to the layperson as a stunning display of frilly parrot petals, dramatic stripes, or bold new combinations of colors. But to the breeder, it is the moment of truth when impossible decisions must be made. After their trial flowers are hand-pollinated, another year must pass for the results to unfold. Sadly, some of these test tulips must be culled to make room for ones that are more worthy of further development. The tulips that remain are

KUNST DER WERELD   JAPAN   ELSEVIER

De Gouden Bocht
van Amsterdam

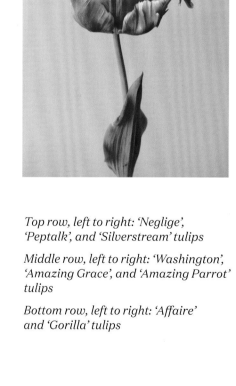

Top row, left to right: 'Neglige',
'Peptalk', and 'Silverstream' tulips

Middle row, left to right: 'Washington',
'Amazing Grace', and 'Amazing Parrot'
tulips

Bottom row, left to right: 'Affaire'
and 'Gorilla' tulips

the lucky ones that live to see another year and perhaps eventually become the next big hit of the flower market. It requires anywhere from ten to fifteen years to develop a new tulip and another five years for it to become eligible for sale. Before a new cultivar can be introduced to the market, extensive inspection, approval, and licensing must be completed.

When a tulip is finally chosen for commercial cultivation, large plots of land are reserved to propagate and build up inventory. Each year, vegetable farmers, breeders, and growers rotate their land use among one another to maintain the fertility of the soil and avoid pest infestations. It is only every few years that growers may be able to cultivate their specialties in their own fields! Completing this challenging puzzle is a testament to the dedication Dutch growers have for sustainability and a willingness to collaborate.

Once the tulip bulbs have bloomed, it is off with their heads! This ruthless but necessary sacrifice happens every April and pierces the tender heart of any flower lover who is witness to it. Heavy machinery cuts the blooms of an entire field within minutes, turning a magical carpet woven with color into a dull green blanket. With the beautiful blooms lying lifeless on the ground, the plant's energy can be redirected back into the bulb so that it will grow to the appropriate harvest size by early summer.

The best time to buy tulip bulbs is from August to December, although outside of the Netherlands, it may be necessary to preorder your favorites earlier in the year to get what you want. Always purchase bulbs from a reputable supplier to avoid any unpleasant surprises. There is nothing more disappointing than your soft pink tulip blooming a bright red come springtime!

Coveted 'La Belle Epoque' tulip combined with playful fritillaria present a reserved but elegant and timeless composition.

PART II

At Home

The history and context of my home are inextricably linked to my work. From my extensive delftware collection and the kitchen sink where I compose arrangements, to the countertop where I sculpt sugar flowers, this domestic space that is my atelier nurtures many creative possibilities. It is important to not only carve out the time but also the space to make fresh floral arrangements and prepare for the life-changing process of sculpting flowers in sugar. Don't be discouraged by thinking a large, sprawling studio is needed to begin sculpting flowers in sugar or arranging them into unique blue-and-white vases. A small space set aside to collect objects of unique craftsmanship will surround you with inspiration to hone your own skills. It is where you can work with light and create composition to capture your subject in photographs.

CHAPTER TWO

Delftware

Delftware is one of the most unique styles of pottery to have emerged from Europe, with striking blue-and-white designs that have become truly iconic. It is a symbol of pride for the Dutch, and more than four hundred years of history can be traced through its development, beginning in the seventeenth century and lasting up until today. Together with famous painters, such as Rachel Ruysch, Rembrandt, and Vermeer, antique delftware is highly valued internationally as a symbol of Dutch art. It is not uncommon for antique delftware to sell for thousands of euros at auction, but equally beautiful and more contemporary pieces can be acquired at a fraction of the cost.

Delftware is deeply connected to the narrative of sugar production and flower arranging. It is no surprise then that I have an addiction to blue-and-white pottery, a condition from which I hope to never recover!

I don't know when it started, but it has permeated every aspect of my life. I have even been known to abruptly gasp "Stop the car!" to my husband when a piece in a shop window catches my eye. This iconic form of pottery has become a blue-and-white lifestyle that now surrounds me at every moment. The colors complement nearly any combination of flowers, and the act of carefully choosing each piece for an arrangement or table setting is a simple way to provide some cheer to everyday life.

My Blue-and-White Addiction

The exact moment when I surrendered to the spell of blue-and-white pottery continues to elude me. Was it the antique delftware plate that I once saw at an aunt's house? As my collection of delftware has grown, its use and presence in my home is a lifestyle that influences every moment: from setting the table for a family dinner, to choosing dinner plates for a gathering of friends, to arranging flowers in a vessel. These pieces guide my daily activities and decorative decisions. Even that first cup of coffee in the morning savored from my favorite blue-and-white cup is a moment of great delight that I never take for granted. Carefully choosing each piece is a simple way to consider how the details of handmade objects can make even the most common rituals something truly special. Because this love for delftware runs so deep, it has influenced many different decorative aspects of our home. From the walls and the curtains to the sofa, the thematic cohesion of a blue backdrop makes my delftware collection pop even more.

Our home inspires me on so many levels. From these blue-and-white objects to flowers and books, it is filled with objects that I love and that make me stop, think, admire, and sometimes become energized throughout the day. I met my husband later in life, and we are both avid collectors of the arts. This made it necessary for me to pare down and be selective about what to keep in our shared spaces. Although I will always admire and collect delftware, I have learned that it is important not to be too distracted by objects that do not provide inspiration. Occasional purging of items is just as gratifying as bringing in new ones.

Historic Beginnings

Delftware has caught and held the love and attention of many from all over the world for centuries. What started out as exclusive pieces for royalty and nobility now has a more accessible path to acquisition and widespread appeal. At the end of the sixteenth century, one of the first Dutch East India Company ships arriving in Holland from China carried precious Chinese porcelain called *qīng-huā* (青花) that had been produced in blue-and-white designs in China for over one thousand years. Ming blue-and-white porcelain wares became so coveted by royalty in the Middle East and Europe that large collections accumulated. The Topkapi Palace in Istanbul housed a stunning assortment of Chinese porcelain belonging to Ottoman sultans; the king of Poland, Augustus II "The Strong," displayed his impressive collection of more than twenty thousand pieces of Chinese and Japanese porcelain in his Japanese Palace in Dresden. But because of the expense and rarity of the originals, potters from the city of Delft began making copies to keep up with demand, and delftware was created as a more affordable and stylish earthenware alternative in Holland.

Porcelain typically consists of large amounts of kaolin clay, but this key ingredient was not accessible in Europe at the time. As a substitute, tin-glazed pottery with milky opacity was painted in a blue-and-white style that mimicked the Chinese porcelain with great precision. As Dutch artisans perfected their new craft, delftware became a must-have for royalty, nobility, and the growing group of prosperous bourgeoisie who needed servingware and decorative objects for entertaining. Elsewhere in the Netherlands and other parts of Europe, similar types of pottery were also beginning to be produced. The Chinese porcelain export market had long been protective of its intellectual property, and great lengths were taken by the Chinese imperial court to avoid having their blue-and-white secrets revealed. Despite this, Chinese porcelain exports declined due to political unrest and trade disruptions between the East and West during the fall and aftermath of the Ming period.

The Influence of Queen Mary Stuart II and King William of Orange III

Queen Mary was an influential tastemaker in her time who steered the style and production of delftware. She was one of the first who displayed flowers in her home in the same way we do today, except that in her case, home meant the most stunning palaces in Europe. Before the seventeenth century, flowers were sometimes used as table decoration for banquets, but were mainly used as garlands in churches to honor God or, in the case of the Greeks, multiple goddesses and gods. Because of her love for gardening and deep admiration of flowers, Queen Mary brought the outdoors inside for the sake of beauty and admiration and did so with a sense of floral design unlike anyone before.

Born in England in 1662 as the eldest daughter of James, Duke of York, and his first wife Anne Hyde, she married her cousin King William III of Holland in 1677 at the age of fifteen and relocated to the Netherlands shortly thereafter. It is questionable whether this royal union was romantically matched, but it was certainly a powerful political play that repaired relations between England and the Netherlands following the Anglo-Dutch War. The couple lived and traveled between Holland and England for the duration of their reign.

It was most likely from a very young age that Queen Mary became passionate about flowers. When she arrived in the Netherlands, her newlywed husband asked his head gardener of Huis Honselaarsdijk (his country estate in southern Holland) to bring into bloom "all the plants, bulbs and seeds of flowers made available to him now and in the future and possibly in every season" so that "[h]e can every week make from the same two or three bouquets for the use of her highness." It is no surprise that William's attempts to woo Mary combined with her appetite for floral beauty resulted in a collection of exotic plants that was one of the largest in Europe. Her fervor was certainly to the benefit of her husband, as their extraordinary palace gardens enhanced his political status. The House of Orange, to which William and Mary belonged, greatly influenced our modern way of gardening and flower arranging. Together, William and Mary redesigned and transformed Het Loo Palace in Apeldoorn, Netherlands, and Hampton Court in London, England.

Under Mary's popular reign, potters in Delft introduced vases with spouts whose designs were perfectly suitable for the placement of rare flowers and plants. Gardeners and botanists working at the court of William and Mary were sent on Dutch East India ships to faraway places to collect the rarest specimens. Hampton Court accumulated about four hundred rare plants that had never been seen in Europe. Vessels were needed at the palace to hold and display stunning arrangements of these plants and blooms, in addition to the ones being grown in their gardens. Numerous large delftware urns, sizable pyramid spout vases, and plates were acquired by Mary to decorate the interior of Het Loo Palace and Kensington Palace and Hampton Court Palace in London.

By the eighteenth century, the demand for delftware had grown so much that there were thirty-four potteries in and around Delft. The industry replaced the textile factories and beer breweries to become the backbone of the Delft economy. But from the early nineteenth century onward, mass-produced, cheaper, and more durable English-made creamware ceramics and porcelain began to rise in popularity. The number of Dutch workshops began to decline by around 1800 due to this competition, combined with poor economic circumstances. The industry experienced a revival in the late nineteenth century, led by De Porceleyne Fles (The Porcelain Jar), which since 1851 had been the only remaining pottery in Delft. There are now only a few pottery factories in the Netherlands that produce porcelain.

The Fabrication of Delftware Pottery

At the height of popularity of delftware, a single pottery was more like a highly organized, bustling factory than the romantic notion of a studio run by a master potter with a few apprentices. Sprawling complexes of workrooms, woodsheds, drying lofts, kilns, warehouses, the pottery owner's home, and a showroom could be found dotted in and around Delft. Each piece of delftware would take as long as two weeks to create, and multiple steps of production were performed by many specialized workers.

Making delftware is a unique and complex process, and it is surprising that these clear blue and sparkling white pieces begin with dull black and white surfaces. First, clay dug from local sources was mixed with clay from neighboring regions and marl (lime-rich mudstone) from Flanders, Belgium. The result was a medium more fragile than porcelain once fired but suitable for blue-and-white embellishment. After mixing, it was purified using tray sieves before being dried and cut into blocks, a laborious series of steps to remove debris. It was then distributed to the potteries, where earth treaders would knead the clay using their feet to make it pliable again for the potter's wheel.

Potters then threw and shaped the clay into various objects, then left their creations for days in drying lofts. Stokers fired large kilns with wood, where the objects would be vitrified in a bisque firing before an underglaze was applied. Specialized painters finished each piece with elaborate and detailed motifs in a paint-like black glaze whose main ingredient was cobalt oxide. Since the famous blue pigment appears only after the second firing, the artisan needed a strong familiarity with the results to bring their intended vision to life with the brush. If other embellishments were made with a red glaze or gold gilding, these would be applied before a third and final low-temperature firing.

Acquiring Delftware

Precious delftware pottery made between the seventeenth century and the first half of the nineteenth century is of incredible value, and most of my personal collection is from the twentieth century. With our young children playing in our home, I would be subject to continuous stress if in possession of pricelessly fragile antiques. Each piece I own, however, has a unique story that makes me appreciate it even more. Some have been presents on my birthday, and others were bought at a heated auction where I hoped to be the highest bidder before going broke! I have even been lucky to discover rare and highly collectible vessels tucked away at a flea market close to my home. Always on a quest to find something new, I love the hunt for delftware at my local flea market. Sometimes I bring cookies to the vendors just to let them know how happy a new acquisition makes me feel.

Living in the Netherlands allows me to be close to the source of exquisite choices, as there are quite a few boutiques specializing in delftware located in Amsterdam. Unfortunately (and understandably because of high rents), the prices in these shops are significantly higher than those at flea markets or online auctions (see Resources, page 238).

When searching for delftware vessels old or new, it is easy to get swept away by the rarity of these treasures—stay realistic and set yourself a budget!

Robert Aronson, who has become a good friend, is one of the most well-known experts on delftware. He has studied their identification, history, and use with detail. He is invited by collectors and museums from all over the world to offer his expertise on unraveling the story of delftware. He says that if you find a piece that feels light and brittle when held in the hand (like an empty milk carton), you may have hit the jackpot! Look for a signature mark on the bottom of a vessel or plate that represents the manufacturer and the year of production. In addition to these details, many factors can influence the price, including whether the blue-and-white motif is hand-painted or stenciled on during production and if there are fine cracks or chips.

Using Delftware for Flower Arranging

Always choose the vase first before arranging flowers. A general rule is to assume a vase should occupy a third of the overall arrangement, with the flowers the remaining two thirds of the presentation. However, sometimes I get carried away and end up with a vase that is only a quarter the size of the arrangement. Because cut flowers were considered special when these vessels were originally produced to hold them, many delftware vases were designed to display only a few precious blossoms. Footed delftware vessels that can display a large arrangement are difficult to find, but their extra height allows the flowers to spill over in a most attractive way. Where the rim is wide, the blooms can be arranged in a loose and spontaneous composition. It is even more special to find a piece in the shape of an urn with plenty of space to hold elaborate bouquets. Although rare, these vessels do exist, and the urn-shaped vases I have collected are most certainly my favorites. As a wonderful alternative, a bowl placed on a cake stand can substitute for the desirable but elusive urn.

Ginger jars filled with flowers with their lid placed nearby can re-create a playful still-life atmosphere. These jars can be quite large and become remarkably heavy when filled with water. To avoid catastrophe, make certain that the table where your arrangement will sit can hold the weight of your water-filled vase.

Clearly, I am an enthusiast of using delftware for flower arranging, but I have learned the hard way that not every delftware vessel is suitable or watertight. I was once nearly brought to tears when I discovered water pouring through the glaze of a new addition to my collection. Another unpleasant surprise was having a mark left on a table because the bottom of a vessel was porous. One clever way to avoid these problems is to place a glass vase and a frog, if necessary, inside a compromised vessel before filling it with water.

Caring for Delftware

Delftware, like other earthenware, is fired at lower temperatures than porcelain, meaning the clay particles are only partly fused together. Because of its porous nature, it is important to be particularly considerate with the maintenance of delftware. Remember that it is prone to staining because liquids can penetrate the body through the pores. When cleaning delftware, use only lukewarm water and a mild soap, if necessary, and dry thoroughly after rinsing. Some glazes and gilding are fired at a relatively low temperature compared with other pottery, such as stoneware or porcelain. This makes them vulnerable to abrasion by repeated cleaning.

CHAPTER THREE

Flowers for Living and Entertaining

Nothing sets the mood quite like an overflowing arrangement nestled beside a generous display of fruit, or a tablescape of late-season dahlias for the Thanksgiving holiday. A home with flowers gives it a soul and undoubtedly adds joy to any room, making it a special place in which to spend quality time alone or with family. When you are creating with company in mind, a few careful considerations will ensure your guests will be welcomed by your creations without unnecessary distraction. I encourage you to consider decorative details so that once your guests arrive, they can relax into the pleasure of your special invitation. Your creations can make anyone feel valued by the gift of your time and thoughtfulness. Set the table in advance with place settings, flowers, and fruit. Any insecurities in cooking prowess don't matter when your guests are swept away by the theater of flowers!

Simplicity

Enjoyment of an arrangement does not have to be about quantity of flowers but rather a respect for nature and working with the resources, financial or otherwise, that are beneficial to you. When decorating the home, never underestimate the impact of one stem or flower. A single bud vase with one perfect marigold cultivated by my daughter in her school garden is still one of my fondest memories. Large displays of grandiosity are a dream for most of us but are not always practical for many reasons. A single bloom with an intoxicating fragrance at your writing desk or a small posy on the dinner table can offer just as much intrigue as large, opulent arrangements.

Creating something out of nothing is its own art form. Regardless of what is most accessible to your location or wallet, you are worthy of welcoming beautiful blooms into your life. Flowers bought at the supermarket, cut short, and arranged in your favorite vessel can be just as captivating as large-scale arrangements spilling over sizable urns. If flowers are difficult to find, use foliage and greens or fresh herbs to decorate a table for a simple, clean, and contemporary look.

Discovering the Language of Flowers

Flowers as companions in our daily activities can brighten our lives, provide comfort, and make a house feel like a soulful, heavenly home. Living with flowers integrates the rhythms of the natural world into our modern lives, even if we do not have a garden or time to stroll in the woods. Bringing the outside in can initiate a hopeful feeling of the promise of spring, celebrate gratitude for summer's endless sunshine, or create a cozy mood during the transience of fall or the hibernation of winter.

The entire process of collecting and arranging flowers awakens the senses and connects you to their emblematic meaning. Whether you are growing and harvesting your own tulips or getting to know vendors at the market, the appreciation you develop for their value only deepens with the personal investment of time. As you choose the vase, practice expanding and contracting your focus on its unique characteristics and the flowers as you fill it. This exercise can provide a great sense of satisfaction, especially when accompanied by a cup of tea for an enjoyable slow-paced afternoon.

The Gift of Time

Few things make me feel as rich as having friends over for dinner. This is when I put forth my best efforts while making precious memories. What is better than sincere conversations surrounded by floral decor and delightful food? Welcoming friends with a beautifully set table is like giving them a present upon their arrival. It makes those we love and admire feel special when you have done your best to reflect their preferences. The best gift you can give someone is not a thing or a beautiful object but rather your time, as it is scarcer than money. A home-cooked meal accompanied by gorgeous flowers is a truly valuable offering.

Welcoming guests with blooms at their full potential, or ready to burst open while in the company of your party, provides the ultimate atmosphere for sensory pleasure. If purchasing cut flowers well in advance of your event, ask the vendor for the estimated vase life to determine if they are suitable and pivot to another vendor if necessary. Sometimes juggling flowers in various holding vases or locations can help manipulate the progression of their opening. To extend the life of flowers, keep them in a cooler spot (such as a basement) to decrease exposure to light and warmth that encourages blooms to open or wilt faster.

Artichokes make a bold statement, whether served as a first course or arranged in a vase with lady's mantle, cornflowers, cosmos, zinnias, and ammi.

Timing

Whether entertaining two, twelve, or twenty guests, careful planning beforehand helps you delight even more in an afternoon or evening with friends. Because of my addiction to flowers, I always start with planning arrangements to fill the entryway, bathrooms, and dining table and prefer setting the table and decorating it with flowers the night before a dinner. This allows peace of mind and the flexibility to tweak anything on the actual day of the event. With decorating out of the way, cooking activities can take center stage. This helps me as the host to relax for the duration of the event.

Setting the Table

Be mindful of using blooms that have a specific scent. For example, the fragrance of hyacinth, lilies, and tuberose can be an unpleasant experience for some, interfering with the enjoyment of culinary pleasures.

I cannot emphasize enough the need to keep table decorations at a low height. There are few things more annoying than conversing around a large arrangement that blocks eye contact or the sound of a guest's voice. Choose a low vessel to accommodate short-stemmed flowers. If you cannot help yourself and decide to sweep guests off their feet with a tall arrangement, consider positioning a smaller table off to the side so you can easily transfer the arrangement while everyone is being seated but still enjoy it throughout the meal.

To create a more intimate space for fewer guests than there are seats, one large arrangement joined by smaller, lower vases with shorter blooms can be scattered throughout the table. The large arrangement can function as a room divider in the middle of the table, and the smaller vases act as company for a small gathering of guests, or when having an intimate dinner with a partner. This way, the rest of the table with empty seats is hardly noticed. Regardless of the size of the gathering, never scrimp on candles for evening celebrations. Candlelight softens the atmosphere and gives everyone in the crowd a gorgeous glow, allowing jewelry and accessories to sparkle.

Double-flowering tulip posies are cheerfully displayed among single tulips in tube vases. Sugar tulips (page 218) nestled on each plate offer keepsakes for guests.

PART III

Creativity

Creativity is the sister of spirituality, an inspired state of being that allows us to connect with something bigger than ourselves and explore our purpose and meaning. When we attune our senses to the moment at hand, it is possible to develop a deeper appreciation for the world around us and live a more fulfilling life. Meaningful connection with our higher purpose naturally leads to emotional well-being, which can alleviate anxiety. For some, it is the best way to fight depression. Living a life of our authentic selves allows us to operate with our hearts and minds united. This state of harmony can have a positive ripple effect on others in our intimate relationships or larger social circles. The magnetism of those in alignment with their purpose is undeniable.

CHAPTER FOUR

Nurturing Intimacy with Nature

The more time we spend developing intimacy with the natural world, the easier it is to feel connected to beauty and bring it into our daily lives. Whether composing a fresh flower arrangement, sculpting a sugar flower, or capturing either in an image, one must first develop an appreciation for the nuances of the plant world before diving into the details of technique. Through careful study and consideration of each petal or rose climbing your neighbor's trellis, you will eventually develop your own language to manifest drama, mystique, romance, and passion in your creations. By studying compositions that evoke emotion and draw attention to color, we can expand our creative practice to embrace and express the lessons of the natural world.

I consider myself fortunate to make a living following my passion. To remain dedicated to clients, it is important to align commissioned work with what can push a creative journey further along its path. Paychecks are important for practical necessities, but we must gift ourselves the freedom to create without consequence. To connect with nature and find a creative flow, include opportunities to explore without an anticipated economic outcome. In those moments without obligation, brilliance can occur.

The Inextricable Beauty of Nature and Art

Opening ourselves to the divinity of flowers can unlock a bottomless well of inspiration. Flowers have long held a place in culture, influencing fashion, design, and literature through their beauty and symbolism. Steven Meisel, Vincent van Gogh, Georgia O'Keeffe, and even Rembrandt with his painting of *Saskia as Flora* are perfect examples of masters captivated and inspired by floral beauty. Tastemaker and New York fashion designer Adam Lippes has even used my floral imagery to create stunning dresses and luxury collections. The olfactory and tactile qualities of fresh blooms along with their associations with love, grief, gender, courage, and much more have figured into a wide range of iconic work. It may seem as if there is nothing new to be said, but the visual and conceptual power of plant symbolism continues to inspire us even today.

The more time you spend studying and creating with flowers, the more you may notice unexpected themes emerging from your work. Nature is the truth teller, and when we surrender to the power of its messages, we become free from unrealistic expectations of the ego and can explore creatively with abandon. The symbolism of plants and the meditative motions of arranging, photographing, or sculpting flowers in sugar are ways to connect to what matters most, even for those without a garden. Studying blooms fosters an acute awareness of the present by clearing the mind and focusing on the beauty at hand. The aesthetic that materializes is a unique expression of your personal experiences and social fabric. Just as nature is dynamic and ever changing, we too are a wilderness of discovering, reflecting, and recombining who we are.

Quiet observation as part of a creative practice can be the beginning of seeing a flower in realistic or abstract potential. When sculpting with sugar, honoring the botanical appearance of flowers will change your relationship with nature and yourself. Re-creating a flower with numerous petals requires patience through the repetition of rolling and sculpting. This exercise may feel challenging and clumsy at first but with time and practice, it will evolve. When we invite serenity into our lives by embracing our talents or limitations, our ability to be kind to ourselves and others greatly expands.

Following Nature's Lead

I am not a big fan of color theories when it comes to flower arranging but prefer instead to surrender to the inspiration that nature provides. Although it is an incredibly helpful tool for some, the color wheel bores me to tears. I resist intellectualizing beauty and avoid abiding by specific rules when arranging flowers. If it is created by nature, it always matches, and there is no need to reject unconventional combinations. We can study, discuss, and intellectualize color but does it really help us creatively? Whether we are presented with plenty of flower choices or only a few, it is important not to feel restricted because of invented rules or popular styles.

Sometimes we simply must make do with what is presented to us when searching for flower gold, and being flexible can prevent unnecessary frustration. One of my favorite arrangements I have ever made used purple, red, and yellow flowers that even I doubted would perform well together in the vase. They were the only blossoms available at the market in good condition, and I was resigned to make it work. With some leftover pops of blue cornflowers from the previous week, stems of fresh citrus, and, of course, a few sugar flowers, I created a fresh and vibrant rhythm that grabbed attention with powerful color combinations and texture contrasts. If I had gone to the market with a wish list or an idealized arrangement, I would not have been nearly as creative. Your work can stand out because of the unexpected. Take risks with daring combinations, as color is a harmless elixir that can truly lift the spirit!

Through this approach, I have built a deep trust in nature's displays of every conceivable color combination that one can imagine. Although we may develop personal preferences over time, defaulting to the wisdom of the natural world means you'll never overthink it. Just as important, always remember that you have the right to change your mind. Intuitive design is a playful dance between the wild and the tamed that often manifests in strong messages of emotion in the vase.

Acceptance and Letting Go

The impermanence of life reminds us that beauty is to be enjoyed in the moment before it is swept away. Nature teaches us that life is always unfolding, and if we embrace the unexpected, opportunities await, even in grief or disappointment. Clinging to a desired result is a burden, but we do not have to operate under fabricated ideals.

For some, striving for perfection in the creative process will always be a struggle. Embracing the irregularities of flowers can help us accept our own shortcomings one bloom or petal at a time. We can become comfortable with uncertainty and let our egos disappear into a world that is bigger and more beautiful than we can imagine.

Blue forget-me-nots tie a riot of spring color together in harmony. Sugar flowers displayed on the table contribute to an enduring still-life ambiance.

CHAPTER FIVE

The Art of Arranging

My style of floral arranging and photography is inherently connected to the location and history of the Netherlands and its former colonies, including the art that resulted as an outpouring of wealth during the global expansion of the Dutch empire. The photographs included in this chapter are examples of compositions that represent a shift in modern objectives, a reinterpretation of affluence that combines exceptional floral beauty with ordinary objects and everyday hospitality. The result is an undeniable atmosphere of *gezellig*, or coziness, especially during time spent with loved ones, but is equally enjoyable in a room of one's own.

Decorating with flowers is a casual expression of the Dutch lifestyle that has evolved over hundreds of years of celebrating prosperity in the home. Although the Netherlands' globalizing ambitions have changed since the Golden Age, and displays of extravagance have become humbler, it is still common for a modern Dutch household to gather friends and family around the pleasures of food, wine, and seasonal blooms reminiscent of celebrated still-life paintings. The timeless works of still-life painters Rachel Ruysch, Clara Peeters, Jan Davidsz de Heem, Jan van Huysum, and Balthasar van der Ast provide an endless source of inspiration that informs and elevates my stylistic process. Elements of still lifes are manifested in my arrangements using complementary objects around the base of the arrangement and flowers in different stages of their life cycle. I will explain the methods and goals of composition when adjusting flowers in an arrangement, and when I use texture to provide contrast. But first, it is worth addressing what results we are trying to achieve by defining beauty.

What Is Beauty?

When practicing any craft that we wish to elevate to artistic expression, it is helpful to first identify goals and priorities. My strongest desire when creating is to achieve an enchanting result that will captivate the viewer. I accomplish this by adjusting the relationship between different branches and blooms, their presence in relationship to the vase and its surroundings, and the light in which the arrangement is enjoyed and photographed. Of course, it is important to consider other factors, such as the audience or the functionality of the arrangement for entertaining, but at the end of the day, a work composed of flowers should be pleasing to the eye.

Everyone will have different opinions about what is beautiful; what is attractive to one person may be jarring or offensive to another. Beauty is certainly subjective, but it is worth addressing what merits praise within an arrangement, photograph, or painting if we are to become better at what we do. There are legitimate differences in tastes and there is plenty of room to disagree with intelligent debate around aesthetics. I would never assert the superiority of one style over another with belittling authority, but I do know what provides me with a sense of satisfaction. I have arrived at these conclusions through life experiences, honing my intuition, and studying the works of esteemed artists whose style calls to me. Inspiration is everywhere!

A beautiful arrangement is the accumulation of nature inspired by dreams, and sometimes expressed honestly by including a gesture of fear or risk. In this sense, it can be a state of aspiration: seeking to capture and elevate what the natural world has to offer. Beauty grabs our attention and captivates us, drawing us into details and nuances of the work. It begs us to question the meaning and intention behind a display created in such a heightened state of rapture. It is honest and profound, and it stirs us. Beauty can provide a brief escape from sadness, and it will always elevate happiness.

Beauty should not be confused with perfection; it embraces irregularities that are inherent in life. An arrangement, a photograph, or a painting can be extremely beguiling because of its imperfections. But when the elements of a composition are assembled, an inherent rhythm and harmony should be evident. The opposite of beauty is not hideousness or ugliness but indifference. The moment we stop feeling, all that is beautiful is lost. It is important to prioritize the heart and keep it open to nurture growth and connection through art.

One of the best ways to hone your eye is to study examples of the Dutch still-life masters. These artists understood ephemerality, and that beauty from the natural world arises from the inevitability of change. Observing their work has made me realize that anticipation, surprise, and longing are inherent in experiencing beauty, but unless it is captured in a painting or photograph, it will never last. Exquisite beauty is often hidden in life's fragile and fleeting moments.

Finding Inspiration in Art

The elements of surprise, moody light, and garden whimsy are all a natural result of my endless quest to bring the joys of the garden inside, to be displayed in arrangements and tabletop settings. To refine my process and become more effective at defining harmony and rhythm, I am constantly turning to the works of Dutch still-life masters whose mastery of composition, defiance of the seasons, and use of symbolism are timeless.

"Still life" is defined as a work of art depicting inanimate and lifeless objects. It comes from the Dutch word *stilleven*, meaning things that lie still. There are various genres of still life, including "breakfast" or "banquet," where the meats, fruit, and porcelain indicate a certain level of economic prosperity, especially if imported. Other categories include *vanitas*, paintings that highlight the futility of earthly pleasure or the folly of wealth during an age of mercantile prosperity and sometimes represent the senseless pursuit of power that led to frequent military conflict. *Vanitas* are closely related to *memento mori*, prompting the viewer to consider their own mortality. These paintings often include skulls, extinguished candles, broken glasses, or even bursting bubbles that suggest the transience of life.

Many of these great painters invented the rules of composition that we still abide by today. When assembling an arrangement, we must consider the path that the viewer's eye will take when observing the finished display. First, consider the position from which the arrangement will be presented: will the viewer be eye level with the display or standing above it, creating angled lines? The shapes that are created by the relationships among flowers or between the finished arrangement and the table display can imply movement or unity. For example, when a triangle is established, so is a sense of balance that is inherently pleasing.

Positioning fruit or sugar flowers at the corners of this triangle momentarily stops the eye to consider the relationship among objects. Selecting one flower, such as an exquisite dahlia or rare stem of fritillaria, to be a focal point is another approach, drawing the eye there first and asking that the other elements of the arrangement become supportive actors; otherwise the composition would appear busy or chaotic. Other approaches to classic compositional styles emphasize strong S-curves or vertical or horizontal lines that, when repeated, establish an undeniable rhythm.

A sense of surprise or a peculiar detail in a Dutch still life sets a predictable, balanced composition apart from an arrangement that is truly special. Including a sugar flower that is out of season strategically in the middle of fresh flowers or a few pops of blue cornflowers among bright pink or orange blossoms halts the eye and begs the viewer to question what is seen. This can be achieved in several other ways, depending upon the plant material that is available. A tall whimsical cosmos towering over a mass of dahlias or a dancing allium stem gyrating to the side of an otherwise demure composition is similarly effective. Just as Rembrandt used the luminous girl in *The Night Watch* (page 95) or Ruysch painted glowing white camellia blooms in *Vaas met Bloemen* (page 21), try to include an unexpected element that will capture the viewers and linger in their memories.

Dutch still lifes highlighted the most rare and exquisite flowers that were available at the time and used them in all stages of their lifespan, including in bud, full and perfect bloom, or a more relaxed fade. Although I love the simplicity of some common flowers, my style is similarly lavish and overflowing; I desire my arrangements and photographs to be like a gift of luxury to the viewer. I begin assembling elements of an arrangement by choosing stems that are unusual, rare, or have wild movement and then supplement

A Dutch still-life-inspired scene overflowing with a lush display of fruits, locally made cheeses, and rustic handmade bread, nuts, olives, and wine for enhancing the pleasures of gathering. The floral arrangement here ties the elements of the tablescape together with height and playfulness and invites the guest to savor delicious seasonal splendor.

with others that enhance their presence. This creates texture within the composition. For example, when working with lilacs, I prefer to fill out the arrangement with other seasonal flowers like tulips that have contrasting forms. This increases each flower's singular worth, and the result becomes something more than the sum of its parts. One plus one can equal so much more than two!

The arrangement style of the Dutch Masters brings attention to colors, textures, and details of flowers including their imperfections. Insect nibbles or tears in a petal can make an arrangement so much more interesting and authentic than greenhouse-grown flowers that may feel stiff or without movement. Don't forget to style your arrangement beyond the vase. Think of how its composition will ask for supplemental or contrasting elements, such as scattered sugar flowers on the table that will hold their vibrancy long beyond those in the vase. The juxtaposition between robust and shapely fruits and the delicate flower petals can also engage the viewer in a lush composition.

The setting and moody light of a Dutch still life are two of the most important elements of evoking this recognizable look. Choose a romantic backdrop of voluptuous drapery, a worn wooden door with character, or textured plaster or paper to manifest ambiance. A blackboard, such as the one in my kitchen, can create contrast and makes the flowers pop. Harsh sunlight will blow out the highlights of flowers and make them look dull, but lower light can bring out the definition of certain elements. Use blinds to diffuse the light of a room where the arrangement will be enjoyed or photographed to keep the colors of the flowers true and make the overall effect subtle. Light coming from one direction will only enhance the drama of the arrangement.

By studying classic still lifes or the work of floral artists inspired by the still-life genre, your eye will become trained over time. With some practice, your process will transition from formulaic to an effortless grace that pleases you.

Snowball viburnum and roses are a base for dramatic tulips and joyful ranunculus. Peony, anemone, and cherry blossom sugar flowers (pages 198 to 227) enhance the Dutch still-life feeling.

Developing a Personal Style

What can I bring to the world when everything has already been done? This question can create self-doubt in inexperienced and seasoned artists alike. Design born from the heart is a unique gift to the world, but it requires confidence and trust in oneself. Personal circumstances and unique experiences shape our creativity in such a way that cannot be replicated. This is reason enough to trust that your own style will emerge if given the opportunity. You will not please everyone, but you will likely stir your audience with a message of authenticity. There is a saying "A flower doesn't think of competing with the flower next to it, it just blooms." To me it is confirmation that we should never let our insecurities or fears hold us back from doing what we love. Creating is a remarkably transformative process and can be about so much more than fabricating an object.

When we wish to set ourselves apart from others, it is necessary to welcome the unconventional and unorthodox. Be bold with color or take risks with composition to discover a formula that is quintessentially yours. If you are unsure of where to begin, looking to the rhythms of nature or even others for inspiration can set you on a compelling path. Most of the Dutch Masters began their hard-earned reputations by working under the tutelage of others and would sometimes practice by replicating their work.

That said, there is a blurry line between being inspired to evoke aesthetic details of others' work and simply copying. The 2019 exhibition "Jean François Millet: Sowing the Seeds of Modern Art" at the Van Gogh Museum featured exquisite works side by side of these two great artists. Van Gogh was greatly inspired by the work of Millet (1814–1875) and some of his paintings were almost identical to Millet's. In a time without internet and little photography, van Gogh would sometimes sketch Millet onto his own canvas. He explained in a letter to his younger brother and art dealer, Theo, in 1889: "And then I improvise color on it, but, being me, not completely of course but seeking memories of their paintings . . . Heaps of people don't copy. Heaps of others do copy—for me, I set myself to it by chance, and I find that it teaches and above all sometimes consoles."

International artists admired Millet's progressive but anti-academic approach, inventive techniques, and use of materials; van Gogh did not stop at copying Millet's work but transformed elements of Millet's paintings and drawings into his own signature style. All creative work builds on what has come before.

Prioritizing the Heart

In my late twenties, after I decided to follow a creative path, my mother casually told me about a conversation she had had with her colleague. The colleague had a teenage daughter and was concerned for her future because she wanted to attend art school. My mother, who would have preferred me to have a more conventional education than fashion school, surprisingly said that the best thing she could do was to encourage her daughter. Although I have always prioritized following my heart, it wasn't without doubt from myself or my loved ones. Hearing this from my mother confirmed that I made the right decision and had become the successful example of a creative professional for my family.

We all have challenges, big and small, that may prevent us from pursuing a creative life and the art of flower arranging. If you find it difficult to set aside time for creativity, begin with a Sunday. When we are caught up in the obligations of work and life in general, this typical day of rest can offer the time and space to do what we love most. If Sunday is not an option, decide which day of the week would be most suitable for you to explore your creative endeavor. If you cannot decide upon a day, then try to incorporate that Sunday feeling into ordinary moments throughout the week.

An urn of viburnum and roses lifts elegant tulips, dramatic fritillaria, textural sweet William, and a sugar rose (page 206) as the focal point. A bud vase and bowl of ranunculus finish the composition.

CHAPTER SIX

Photography

I am a self-taught and permanent student of photography who, out of necessity, learned to record fleeting floral moments in the famous natural light of Amsterdam. Knowing how to compose a photograph and direct the light using either a simple camera phone or a digital single lens reflex camera (DSLR) is helpful for both working with clients and honing your design eye. Composition, contrast, and the manipulation of natural light as they pertain to an image are all important elements in a photograph. Allow yourself to fall in love with each flower as you study the arrangement, noting which ones speak to you and crave attention. Acknowledging what you value in a composition helps you present your subject in its most glorious representation.

Documenting Your Work

Photography is a beneficial tool for honing and sharing your vision for future events or documenting past experiences. Images of flower creations can communicate your passion, whether it be for a client meeting, your website, or social media. It is a way to build a portfolio and set yourself apart from others.

There is no such thing as sharing too much beauty through stunning images. It is rewarding to not only reflect on the beauty of your creations but also to track your creative progress. A professional photographer can be expensive to hire, but with a little practice and some guidance, you can become adept at photographing your work and editing your images. The lens of a camera can explore a world of various perspectives, but great photographers portray what speaks to their own eyes, including what is commonly unnoticed. I treat photography as an art form that has the power to expose or manipulate reality. What I choose to highlight becomes free from the confines of time and place and is more accessible to a wider audience.

From Hobbyist to Professional

Photography is derived from the Greek words *photo*, which means light, and *graphos*, a representation of lines, or to draw. Photography literally translates to "drawing with light." I am neither a skilled sketch artist nor a painter, so I have great admiration for those who can perform either with talent. If you too are unable to express yourself through pen, pencil, or paintbrush, photography may be a more approachable substitute that can provide instant gratification.

My passion for photography began during holidays with my family in Suriname. Narrow coastal plains dotted with swamps and marshes and the rolling hills of the interior covered by tropical rainforests were perfect subjects for my analog Canon camera. When not enthralled with the landscape, I respectfully documented the indigenous community going about their daily activities. Anxious days followed handing in those film rolls, and the reward of flipping through the returned stack of pictures is still a joyful memory. The contemporary world of photography now relies heavily on digital imaging and editing software. There are still photographers who prefer conventional methods, but with digital cameras, we can adjust hundreds of images while styling our subjects without the waste of unnecessary, costly paper. It is possible to become better photographers with the right equipment.

The camera technology of modern phones makes it much easier to record and share important moments with just a few clicks of the finger and provides an accessible entry for those interested in becoming more serious about photography. Each new generation of phone cameras presents the opportunity to create higher-quality results. Everyone can now produce images worth admiring, and it is easier to transform from a hobbyist into a professional with low up-front investment costs. There are even books like *A Wandering Eye* by leading interior photographer Miguel Flores-Vianna that are full of extraordinary images made entirely with a phone.

When I began photographing flowers, I loved working with my iPhone. It was uncomplicated and efficient to create stunning shots for uploading to social media. As I gained a following, I began creating high-resolution photographs for limited edition art prints using a digital single-lens reflex camera (DSLR). However, sophisticated phone camera features make it possible to shoot in raw image file (RAW) for easy adjustments in Adobe Photoshop. Simply tapping on the phone screen to make light adjustments or using portrait mode functions can create beautiful images with depth and clarity. Whether working with a professional or phone camera, focus on what is needed to communicate your message. If an image needs a lot of Photoshop adjustment, consider opting for one whose composition, contrast, and light are better represented.

Composition

Composition in photography is the framing of your image and the placement of your subject within that frame. This is the first step toward creating an impactful image, and without it, you risk omitting key elements. Make sure there is something of interest within the frame that grabs and holds your attention, such as a bloom that is in its most ideal and exquisite stage. Try including a particular object or group of objects that evokes a thought that is pleasant, disturbing, or makes your heart beat a little faster. Identify what the subject is trying to convey, such as the seasons, romance, vibrancy, luxury, or abundance, and make sure the composition communicates your message. For example, an abundance of flowers, especially roses, can exhibit an air of romance, whereas daisies convey innocence and simplicity. The same arrangement may be photographed in dozens of different ways depending upon what you deem most meaningful and compelling. Zooming in on a particular blossom, capturing the full arrangement including the vase, or pulling forward a certain flower to enhance its presence will each result in vastly different images and impressions. Before you snap the photo, take the time to observe attentively and be enchanted with your subject, for it is what your eye notices that matters.

Contrast

Contrast in a photograph draws attention to its subject, creates depth, and directs the viewer to details worth noting. Contrast can be created with black or dark colors against white or light ones, or by working with different textures, as seen on pages 101 and 102. With my camera mounted on my tripod ready to take a photograph, I sometimes refer to old masters' paintings for inspiration. The contrast and light they illustrate attune my eyes to be sensitive to both and help me capture the same in my final frame.

Light

Light is what brings magic to any photograph, and I prefer using natural sources. Even in winter when there is only a short window of time in which to work, studio lights or lamps are no substitute for the soft shadows of morning or evening sunshine. I am fortunate to be surrounded by the famous Dutch light, which shifts frequently throughout the day. Even when it is overcast, only a few minutes of waiting will lift the gloominess and brightness will return. Four seasons in one day are typical conditions in the autumn, and I am constantly chasing the light with my camera as it moves throughout the day. Because of this rhythm to my work, my children and husband have also become more attuned to the sun's movement. When warm rays fill our home, my children will sometimes declare, "Mom, the light is beautiful! You must photograph!"

Creating a permanent spot in your home or studio with natural light helps you capture images with ease, especially during spontaneous moments of inspiration like these. Overhead shoots can especially benefit from the right spot with the most favorable light. As you practice with your camera, notice how the sun and shadows move in your own home or studio. Because we read from left to right, my favorite location for taking pictures is with a window on the left side of the subject. Adjustable soft linen curtains or blinds help regulate and filter the incoming light, particularly if it is harsh or the sun is high. A 5-in-1 collapsible reflector is also helpful to redirect or bounce light or to brighten darker spots in the frame. This light reflector comes with a gold or a silver side to either warm up or cool down colors. I use small handheld mirrors to create reflection or to highlight and emphasize what needs attention. Using different backgrounds of draped natural linen, painted or dyed fabric, paper, or wood can also help create atmosphere and contrast.

Heirloom dahlias basking in the glow of autumn's natural light with dancing stems of Chinese bittersweet and dill.

The Night Watch

One of the most famous of Dutch paintings is *The Night Watch* by Rembrandt van Rijn. I consider it a perfect example of how light, contrast, and composition can harmonize an image. The canvas size is overwhelmingly large, and the way light and shadow are captured is so dramatic, it is simply breathtaking viewed in person. There is so much to admire in this painting, but your eye is immediately drawn to the appearance of the unusual little girl dressed in white, appearing like an angel that illuminates the foreground. The pale costume of the lieutenant (Willem van Ruytenburch) and the hand of the captain (Frans Banninck Cocq) reflect the light and grab the viewer's attention. Everyone is painted against a dark background, but the noticeable contrast spotlights these three characters.

Just like the guardsmen and girl of *The Night Watch*, I consider my flowers characters in a play and note which ones want to take center stage in an arrangement. Are there flowers with a gracefully bent stem that stand out when used in full length? Consider keeping these stems taller, allowing their unique forms to tower over the rest. Which flowers function as supporting actors who emphasize the lead players even more? Using handheld mirrors to redirect and bounce light off a star flower is an effective way of enhancing the star's noticeable attraction. Are there flowers that are remarkable not just in shape but also color? Using a sugar flower to contrast with the supple texture and colors of fresh flowers is another way to draw attention to a focal point or create interest.

It always takes time to be completely satisfied with an arrangement or to compose its photographic image. Styling and tweaking within the photo frame is a continuous, playful dance. Stand back on occasion and note when it is necessary to remove a bloom that blocks the splendid features of another flower behind it. Sometimes it is necessary to prevent dark spots or fill holes in an arrangement, but on occasion, consider welcoming them to add tension and interest to an image.

Rembrandt van Rijn, De Nachtwacht *(*The Night Watch*),*
1642. Rijksmuseum, Amsterdam, the Netherlands.

Equipment

Some of the most iconic photographs have been taken with cameras that are not as specialized as today's technology. Good equipment helps, but it is not a requirement or a guarantee of a good, let alone outstanding, photograph.

Most photographs throughout this book were taken with my Canon EOS 80D camera using a Canon 18-135mm or a Sigma Art lens 18-35mm F1.8. I use a macro lens 105 F2.8 for close-up flower photographs. If you wish to upgrade the equipment you already own, consider investing in extra lenses rather than a brand-new camera. But most important, become comfortable with using your camera in your own way, and do not let technology be an obstacle.

Manual mode helps create more unique photographs than using the automatic function on a camera. Begin by choosing the best ISO setting (the light sensitivity of a camera), then the aperture (lens opening, or F-stop), followed by the shutter speed. Crop in your camera by finding the right angle of your subject and then zoom in by hand. Play with your shutter speed, discover the possibilities of different lens openings, and develop your own favorite settings. Remember: natural light, room or background color, reflection, and the time of day can influence your results but there is no right or wrong way to capture a subject. Experiment, learn, and play with your camera until you achieve the images that please you.

I keep my ISO setting low, preferably between 160 to 400, to achieve better, sharper photographs. This range also suggests the drama, moodiness, and mystery that I strive to convey. I prefer a depth of field to range from aperture F-stop 2 to F-stop 16, which results in clear images overall. Going lower can be appropriate for a specific point of focus or for capturing a detail or object against a blurry background. F-stop 7.1 to 10 is a good stop to start for a sharp focus on your subject balanced with a fading background.

For sharp and clear images, it is worth investing in a stable tripod that leaves your hands free and prevents movement of your camera. For more detailed visibility of your images on a computer screen, consider using a tethering cord to connect your camera to a desktop or laptop nearby.

Photographing Peonies

One of the most challenging flowers to photograph is the peony because it is highly sensitive to warmth and light. The blooms you begin with will look entirely different moments later, unfolding right before your eyes. Buds can open before you know it, especially when transferred from a cool corner to a warm, bright spot close to a window. Keep this in mind when you intend to photograph peonies and set aside more time than you think necessary to capture every riveting moment of their unfolding.

Vulnerability

I was sixteen years old when I learned one of the most important lessons about creativity. I started sewing my own dresses, complete with pleats, neat stitches, and perfectly pressed collars. But there was one essential thing that was always missing: a well-stitched hem that would complete my clothing and deem them wearable. I was so afraid that people would think my clothes were not good enough, I never wanted to reveal them. It wasn't until sometime after attending the school of fashion that I felt validated and confident enough to wear them in public.

When we create, we make ourselves uniquely vulnerable to interpretations and opinions of our work. Although you are holding this book and hopefully enjoying its photographs, it took me a long time to add "photographer" to my job title. It takes courage to arrive at a place of confidence where our light is not dimmed by the criticism of others. It is necessary, however, to push beyond the risk of criticism and face your fears; it only gets easier with time. Celebrate the small victories as you make progress toward developing a signature style. Creating and capturing your most beautiful arrangements should satisfy you first and foremost. Once this is achieved, your message will become easier to communicate to others.

Killing Your Darlings

There are many images that I am proud of, and I even have a few favorites. But I cannot say with certainty that I have ever created what I would consider *the* ultimate photo. Even with hundreds of images to choose from, the most difficult task is to stop and step away at the end of a shoot. There is always room for improvement, and it may feel as if a work is never finished. The light may change suddenly, causing you to notice details in a different way. Or you may rotate the vase a quarter turn and the arrangement assume a new identity that begs for documentation. Choosing the right photograph to share with your audience and leaving behind the others can be an even bigger challenge than knowing when to stop. As the writer Elizabeth Gilbert suggests, perfectionism can murder creativity. The notion of "Done is better than good" guides me often and has prevented me from going mad on more than a few occasions.

PART IV

The Arrangements

Being inspired by flowers beckons us to work with their unique attributes and develop a language that speaks their messages into our daily lives. It doesn't take much space or investment to get started, but a few considerations will help to set up an in-home flower studio and source, forage, and condition live plant material for lasting arrangements. As a bonus, planting and harvesting from a small rooftop terrace or patio can provide that one branch or bloom that may make all the difference in your designs.

Precious red dogwood gifted from a friend's garden is flower gold and provides a colorful base for anemones and tulips. Snippets of elm branches complete the arrangement.

CHAPTER SEVEN

Searching for Flower Gold

Creating gorgeous floral art that inspires admiration is easy with fresh and beautifully preserved plant material. Regardless of where you reside or whether you have a garden, a few straightforward tips for acquiring your treasures will prepare you for a satisfying experience of arranging and enjoying your creations. Setting up a workspace at the home, hunting for gorgeous blooms, and conditioning your flowers for extra-long vase life will let your creativity flow uninterrupted with the most luscious options that are available to you, regardless of your location.

Acquiring a few essential tools and equipment from anchors and floral putty to turntables and buckets will set you on your way to creating stunning floral arrangements. Begin by setting yourself up in an accommodating workspace and choose the appropriate vessels, vases, and containers to cooperate with your intentions. Although flower markets overflowing with bundles of blooms are excellent resources for acquiring plant material, backyard gardens, rooftop terraces, and respectful foraging are all clever ways of collecting inspiration. With time, you will learn what is available to you in your region and friends will gift you their most gorgeous branches, knowing how much you appreciate their beauty.

Seasonality

Almost everything is for sale, and this most certainly applies to flowers. Because of globalization, we can purchase almost any bloom at any time, even peonies in December. As one of my flower vendors explained, "It is always peony season somewhere in this world!" Although this may be true, I strive to honor the seasons when arranging beauty in the vase. The field-grown offerings of spring and summer are not only many, but their stems and flowers are exquisitely unique and can make a big difference on the visual impact in an arrangement.

That said, I respect that when blooms become scarce, we must become more creative with greenhouse-grown blooms. In winter, I am content with the advancing technology of the Netherlands that has not only made seasonal trickery feasible but also sustainable. When there is a lack of abundance or choice, I joyfully embrace this opportunity as well as the allure of sugar flowers, an inspired resource of dignified splendor.

Sourcing

My arrangements have a decadent and overflowing aesthetic at times, no doubt encouraged by the Dutch floral trade that surrounds and caters to my interests in every way. Because most cut flowers originate from the Netherlands, they are less expensive here than elsewhere in the world. I still take time to visit my local growers to source and photograph their flower gold and build lasting relationships. Every spring when tulips are blooming or in autumn when dahlias are still going strong, I take the time to visit their fields. Within an hour's drive of Amsterdam, I can be at the edge of a carpet of color stretching sometimes for miles. It is an overwhelming sensation that every flower lover should experience at least once in their lives.

If you do find yourself in the Netherlands during the growing season, always make appointments before visiting and never enter a field without permission. When photographing a field or sourcing blooms anywhere in the world, early appointments or ones at the end of the day are best. It is always better to cut flowers when the sun is low for prolonged longevity; also, the light at these hours is perfect for photography. Flowers basking in bright sunlight are more difficult to capture and often appear stressed from the heat.

When visiting flower fields, I always bring one or two buckets and recycled plastic bottles filled with water to prevent blooms from wilting after they have been harvested. The one or two initial buckets are my attempt at modesty, but I almost always fail miserably, returning home instead with even more buckets of gifted blooms than I anticipated sourcing.

I am very proud of the significant part the Netherlands takes in the flower industry, but I encourage you to build relationships with your local vendors and growers who create magic in their nurseries. Supporting local flower farms reduces use of fossil fuels and directs resources into building green jobs that support organic practices. This applies not only to cut flowers, but also to bulbs and seeds for growing in your garden. Ask vendors where they get their flowers—you might even encourage them to buy more from local growers. Searching close to home is not only sustainable, but building these relationships truly adds value to the love we all share for flowers.

A ginger jar of roses carries sweet William, ranunculus, and anemone. Daucus carota 'Dara' and a sugar peony (page 198) provide focus and whimsy. Cherry blossoms spill over the rim.

Top row, left to right: 'Bumble Rumble', 'El Paso', 'Fancy Pants', and 'Frost Nip' dahlias

Middle row, left to right: 'Hollyhill Calico', 'Jowey Winnie', 'Kelsey Annie Joy', and 'Maxime' dahlias

Bottom row, left to right: 'Dinnerplate', 'Penhill Watermelon', and 'Tartan' dahlias

A Passion for Local Blooms

Sourcing plant material is so much more than simply finding gorgeous blooms. It is an opportunity to connect with others, be inspired by their motivations, and support a local flower economy centered upon gentle land stewardship. Joshua and Jeremy Scholten are two dear flower friends of mine and brothers who cultivate peonies. One day they called to say that one of my favorites, 'Pastel Elegance', was in bloom and that I should come by to fetch some. We chatted as they cut the stems in their enchanting peony fields while the sun was setting. After they had handed me a gorgeous fistful of buds and flouncy blooms, I asked if they were tired and ready to go home. They answered yes but with the caveat that their work is never finished.

There are never enough hours in a day for the meticulous process of breeding peonies. These brothers are true designers when it comes to cultivating new cultivars, and their dedication to detail is unmatched in the industry. Just one tulip can require up to fifteen years of development before it hits the market, but peonies can take even longer! Color, size, and heavenly perfume are all taken into consideration, and this requires decades of time and commitment. They wouldn't endure sore hands and backs, nor the freezing cold and scorching sun, if they didn't love the land they are stewarding or the flowers they are growing.

The passion that these brothers have for their work is contagious and can energize those who use their blossoms to carry it forward. Although their story may not be known when the arrangement is seen by others, their dedication is communicated through the beauty of the flowers and their impact on your process. Working without economic rewards to chase and create beauty is the ultimate sacrifice for living a life of purpose.

As a bonus, supporting local breeders and farmers often comes with an environmentally friendlier footprint. A wider diversity of flower choices is usually available, and this supports an ecosystem in the field that benefits the birds, bees, and other fauna of the landscape, especially when the flowers are grown organically. These cut flowers almost never leave water and use little wasteful packaging to get them to your studio. The result is blooms cultivated with love and care that have a natural feel and unmatched swagger. They typically last much longer than imported flowers and, just as important, there is a face behind their beauty.

There are several flower vendors whom I visit each Saturday at our open-air market and who all offer a different selection of flowers. Seeing their stalls filled with an abundance of flower gold is always a thrill, and I look forward to seeing each one for a chat as much as purchasing the blooms. We have learned one another's preferences so well that sometimes they will even message a heads-up if they have found something rare.

These vendors make a tremendous effort to find the best flowers at the right price. Most customers want to buy as much flower beauty as they can for the cheapest price, without consideration for the work that goes into these blooms. Flowers require an incredible amount of manual labor and natural resources, and this is passed on to each person in the supply chain before they arrive in your home or studio. Purchasing flowers at your local flower shop may bring a higher bill compared with the local market, but shop owners are burdened with monthly obligations like higher rents.

Wholesale vendors are another option to explore if you are eligible to purchase at these venues. When buying from a wholesaler, we may not know the backstory of where these flowers originate or under what conditions. The best we can do is identify our priorities or needs and make decisions accordingly.

Market Etiquette

"Can I take a photograph?" is a common request by tourists and others captivated by the abundant display of flowers at the market. I have often witnessed this interaction as a bystander and most flower vendors kindly oblige. One vendor once mentioned with a sigh, "If I received a euro each time someone asked to photograph my flowers, I would be rich by now!" Consider buying a bloom when you are granted a photo of lush flower gold and resist handling the blooms on offer that you do not intend to purchase. Buckets filled with flowers seemingly crave attention and are incredibly tempting to touch. Like the endearing sight of a baby, the squidgy soft appearance of blooms brings out our reflex to squeeze and caress them. The stems of poppies, scabiosa, and clematis, however, are prone to bruise or snap when touched on their flower heads. Always be careful when choosing bunches for yourself or, better yet, leave this selection to your vendor.

On Being Resourceful

Trucks filled with greenery pruned from the private gardens of Amsterdam have made me hit the brakes and turn around in pursuit of this incomparable resource. With permission of the gardeners, stunning vines and grape leaves have made their way into my arrangements on more than one occasion. One person's waste is sometimes another person's treasure! Seeing the beauty in the most unassuming trimmings or weeds can sometimes make an arrangement extraordinary.

If you are searching for inspiration for sugar-flower sculpting, it is not always possible to have fresh blooms at your disposal and photographs can be second-best options. Thankfully most of us have a camera on our phones, allowing the opportunity to capture flowers in the park or along a private fencerow.

Friends and family are familiar by now with my floral passion, and some of them with gardens have gifted me stunning specimens of color, form, and texture. It is important to remain open to all possibilities when searching for flower gold, and welcoming flowers into your life can look very different depending upon your location and resources. The magic of creating a dialogue with the natural world means that surprise beauty can appear when it is least expected!

Making Flower Friends

I am so grateful for the people who enhance the beauty of Amsterdam by growing bulbs in pots and cultivating blooms on trellises at their doorsteps. Some of these plants are difficult to find as cut stems but are perfect for re-creating in sugar. Camellias are a stunning example, but cultivating these large shrubs is unrealistic for many. I have a few fledgling camellias potted on my rooftop but, thankfully, there is an even larger bush growing nearby our home. Sometimes in winter, I take a detour just to admire when they are in bloom. I am known in my neighborhood to occasionally ring a doorbell, even at the risk of being perceived as a crazy flower lady. I usually take my chances anyway and ask if it is okay to snip a bloom.

I made this unusual request once of someone whose door was overgrown with heirloom roses. Their dreamy irregular petals are not often found in commercially grown roses, and I knew they would dance in the vase. When I explained that I needed only one or two to create flowers in sugar, the owner's curiosity was provoked, and permission was granted willingly. Sometimes I pay a return visit to these generous souls with the finished product that leaves them in awe of the flower's sweet immortality. Making new friends through the shared appreciation of flowers contributes to a sense of community and makes us more appreciative of the natural world in all its beautiful forms.

Planting Without a Garden

It seems nearly everyone who loves flowers dreams of having their own garden, especially floral artists who appreciate the relaxed forms of homegrown blooms and branches. Although the Netherlands is known for its enormous displays of bulbs in the millions, urban dwellers have many fewer options. I have lived my whole life in a city without an in-ground garden and consider those that have one fortunate to have true wealth in their lives. Instead of considering this a setback, I have packed every meter of our rooftop with plants, tucking bulbs into pots and wedging hydrangeas into tight corners with the hope that one day I will have a more expansive space to call my own.

Rather than lamenting our fate, this lack of land has deepened my appreciation of what we are so lucky to have and encouraged me to invest in our wonderful rooftop terrace. However, the urge to grow more than what I can fit into its footprint has never left me and may be a similar situation to yours. With limited space, I have had to learn restraint and to maximize the possibilities. I keep a calendar of planting and gathering times to stay organized; not many things in life leave me yearning, but ordering tulip bulbs brings out an intense desire for growing more. Even if you have room for only one pot, you can still make clever decisions with a little thoughtful planning. For example, choosing early- as well as late-blooming bulbs will prolong the glorious and joyful tulip season.

I am lucky to have relationships with plant breeders who suggest the bulbs or plants that are most suitable for growing in pots. Consult with a reputable nursery instead and build relationships that over time can be immensely helpful in maintaining your plants. For example, not every herbaceous peony can be grown successfully in a pot; those that can require ample soil depth and excellent drainage. The stunning pink peony 'Doctor Alexander Fleming' is thankfully sturdy enough to thrive on my windy rooftop as well as the clear white-to-cream and slightly fragrant 'Madame Claude Tain'. As a rule, providing ample root depth for most perennials, shrubs, and especially tulips will lead to healthier plants and more impressive flowers.

This calendar features some of the annuals, perennials, and shrubs that I can successfully grow in pots throughout the year, and I hope it encourages you to make a similar plan of your own. Many of the plants listed are a onetime investment and, with attention to soil fertility and proper watering, will allow you to reap their rewards for years to come. Just one or two of these stems can sometimes make an arrangement extra special, an encouragement for those with little experience in gardening. If ever there is outdoor space left untouched, turning it into a small potted garden will surprise you with stunning floral offerings.

My mild maritime climate can nurture a wide diversity of plants and is equivalent to the USDA hardiness zone 8b. With some rich, well-draining soil, ample sunshine, and a consistent water source, anyone can celebrate the luxury of exceptional or even

	SPRING	SUMMER	AUTUMN	WINTER
PERENNIAL				
Hellebores				<Blooming > Gather
Camellias				<Gather >
Geum	Plant <Blooming >			
Primula	<Blooming>			
Iris	Plant bulbs <Blooming >			
Peony		<Blooming >	Compost	
Roses		Compost Deadheading		Prune and plant
Passion flower		<Blooming >		
Clematis	Prune <Blooming >			
Wisteria	<Blooming > Prune			
Jasmin	<Blooming >			
Lilly of the valley	(Plant)		(Plant)	
Hostas	< Plant all year Blooming >			
Lilacs	<Blooming > Prune			
Foxglove	<Blooming >			
Japanese anemone		<Gather >		
Hydrangea	<Blooming >			Prune
ANNUAL				
Amaryllis			Order Bulbs	
Daffodill	Harvest Gather	(pre) order Bulbs	Plant Bulbs	
Tulips	Harvest Gather		Plant Bulbs	
Sweet peas	Blooming			Plant or sow
Cosmos		<Gather >		
Dahlias	Plant tubers	Gather	<Remove tubers>	Order new tubers

rare flowers grown in a small container garden on a patio, small balcony, or rooftop terrace. Heirloom roses with graceful stems, specialty tulips, dainty fritillaria, or smoky hellebores will generously return love and care with gifts of unique color, form, and texture. If you fancy bringing some inside for a brief floral display (such as the 'Bridal Crown' daffodil featured opposite), try planting them in small decorative pots or plastic containers that you can slip inside more precious collectible pottery when they are ready to bloom. With just one or two or even an abundance of pots, our hands in the soil keep us connected to the seasons and grounded in the cycles of life, even when we are standing on rooftops high above the earth.

Setting Up a Flower Studio

One needs very little space or equipment to relax, reflect, and awaken the senses while working with flowers. Using what you have available to nurture tranquility allows your mind to relax and what manifests in the vase, in sugar, or in a photograph to flow naturally. What will result is an authentic expression of your inspiration and an innate response to the moment at hand. Acquiring a few tools and techniques are all that is necessary to nurture the inner dialogue between yourself and the natural world.

When I designed bridal couture for private clients, I had a studio in the heart of Amsterdam, but it became increasingly difficult to spend time there once my children were born. Not being physically present for their needs and the monthly obligation

of high rent eventually led me to create a studio in the space where I am fortunate to call home. I had some feelings of failure but was mostly relieved when I ended my lease after more than fifteen years.

I have always dreamed of having a flower room equivalent to those in stunning English castles. It would be a stately room with tall windows overlooking magnificent cutting gardens and a large sink to keep everything clean. The walls would be lined with shelves filled with various vessels, and all my equipment would have its place. Stunning arrangements created in such a magical studio would be transferred to living spaces, libraries, and bedrooms for my family and guests to enjoy.

We cannot change something (or someone) that makes us unhappy. Fortunately, we *can* control our attitude and perception of people and events to feel less affected. This piece of wisdom has been invaluable throughout my life, but especially as a creative professional. The physical dimensions of my canal home cannot be altered to suit my wildest castle dreams, but my perception of how to experience them can be.

To come as close to my dream of a flower room as I could, I sacrificed part of our kitchen and an adjacent light-filled sitting room. In addition, the bathroom and bathtub have become the perfect space to rinse and clean large vases. Our marble kitchen countertop has become the perfect workplace, and I spend much time in our kitchen using it. Once I began making sugar flowers, I cleared out some cabinets and filled them with sculpting equipment while reserving a prominent space for my stand mixer. Baking cakes and creating sugar flowers consumed me from that moment on. It took me some time to reorganize, but consciously creating space for tools and equipment was a very rewarding process. Whether I have deliveries for clients, a private class, or a photography assignment, our home has become a place of productivity and creative inspiration.

Equipment

These simple tools will make it easy to compose creative arrangements and welcome the most beautiful flower gold into your studio no matter its size or source. The key is to own and maintain these tools in a way that can assist in effectively cutting, conditioning, and anchoring stems into any size vessel.

Pin frogs

Floral putty

Floral scissors, various sizes

Pruning shears

Sharp knife

Chicken wire

Wire cutters

Cellophane tape (clear masking tape)

Turntable

Floral wire

Anchoring Plant Material

The most marvelous invention for securing stems and branches in an arrangement is the pin frog (also known as flower frog or frog, for short) or *kenzan*, as its known in Japan. It was originally designed to execute the Japanese floral art of ikebana and works marvelously for holding stems of all sizes upright in a vase. Even when there are only a few stems in a small vase, a small pin frog will create support and help you adjust the position of every bloom.

Pin frogs come in all sizes, shapes, and forms, and many are highly collectible. I have a large assortment of vintage frogs that I have collected over the years. Some were sourced secondhand on Marktplaats, the Dutch equivalent of eBay, and others I was given by my dear friend Hannette, who inherited them from her mother-in-law. Most well-made frogs are of heirloom quality, and I consider myself their caretaker until they are passed on to the next generation of floral artists.

To use a pin frog, ensure both your vase and the frog are free from moisture that would undermine the floral putty and cause it to slide. If using a spiky metal pin frog, wear garden gloves or use a folded towel to protect your fingers. Cut a generous amount of floral putty from its roll and stick the putty to the bottom of the frog in a twisted fashion. Place the frog, putty side down, onto the bottom of the vase. Give it a slight twist to secure it in place.

It is both frugal and sustainable to reuse the same pin frog and its putty. To remove the pin frog and putty from the vase, use a folded cloth to protect your fingers from the pins and gently twist and wiggle them free. Hold the frog and the attached putty under streaming warm-to-hot water to soften and separate the putty, being mindful of the metal becoming hot in your hands. Use a brush with soap to clean the sharp pins and allow both the frog and floral putty to dry completely before reusing.

For additional support of heavy branches or for wide-mouthed vases, a chicken wire cushion nestled inside the vase and secured with cellophane tape (clear masking tape) to the rim is easy and inexpensive to make. Wearing protective gloves, cut a piece of chicken wire almost twice the height of your vase and scrunch the ends under to form a rounded dome. The dome needs to rest about an inch above the rim of the vase. Secure it inside the vase over a pin frog with a grid of clear masking tape stretched over the rim of the vase (pictured on page 170). Remove and reuse these cushions repeatedly, washing with a sponge, soap, and warm water before they are left to dry.

Pin frogs and chicken wire cushions are valuable and more sustainable solutions than petroleum-based, nonbiodegradable, and nonrecyclable floral foam.

Floral wire comes in different thicknesses ranging from 16-gauge to 33-gauge and is excellent at providing hollow stems with extra support. The lower the gauge number, the thicker the wire, but it is most common to use 18-gauge for maximum support and 20-gauge for subtle support. When inserting the wire through the stem, stop before piercing the flower. Ranunculus, poppies, anemones, and gerbera daisies are just a few flowers that benefit from this technique. Even when the stems are strong, I sometimes use a wire to help control their direction, especially during a photography session. Hearing what a plant is speaking to a composition is an important skill to cultivate in floral artistry, but sometimes it is helpful to have some subtle control over your material.

Turntables

Although I do not always work on a turntable (also known as a lazy Susan), it is remarkably helpful for considering an arrangement that will be viewed from all sides. This invaluable tool will not only assist in identifying empty spaces but also helps when composing large or complex compositions.

Conditioning Cut Flowers

Returning from the market with bunches of blooms can inspire you to get lost in their beauty. Taking a pause is helpful before settling into creative mode, and luckily, conditioning flowers in glass vases allows extra time to get organized. This post-harvest care begins with the grower and should continue once the stems reach your studio. Although each plant may appreciate specific treatments, taking the necessary steps to let the flowers gather strength before arranging will extend their lives in the vase. Simply put, ensure the stems are cut at a diagonal to uptake plenty of water. Be sensitive to temperature changes that can traumatize flowers, and ensure your vessels and water are sparkling clean. Except for tulips (see tips below), stripping bottom leaves discourages their decay in the water, a step that should become instinctive over time. If purchasing directly from flower farms, be mindful of soil that may still be clinging to the stems after harvest and rinse well to avoid contamination.

Use heavy glass vases to hold your thirsty specimens until they plump up before they are arranged in a more decorative vessel. Glass vases are not porous, which makes it easier to eliminate bacteria by cleaning them with soap and warm or hot water. Always be careful when using hot water in combination with glass to avoid unwanted damage or cracks. If you would hesitate to drink from your vessel, give it another scrub. Various sizes of glass vases are ideal and provide a choice for supporting smaller, delicate blooms or large, heavy branches.

Branch and Flower Stem Treatments

"What music were you playing in the background?" was the reply given to me by my vendor when I complained that the peonies I bought from him the week before did not open. Struck for a moment by his reply, we both burst out in laughter. Sometimes flowers do not perform in the way we would want them to (regardless of their background music), but there are some things we can do to prolong the longevity of their vase life.

Every flower should ideally be conditioned in its own way before it is gathered into arrangements. The amount of time conditioning takes will depend upon how the stems were harvested, how long they have been cut, and temperature and light exposure of where they are conditioned. Conditioning can take from a few hours to overnight before flowers look visually refreshed, but it will ensure they last longer in the vase. Over time you will learn how each type of stem appreciates being handled, but the following are some tips and tricks for commonly used plant material.

- Soft, fleshy, and herbaceous stems generally need to be conditioned in tepid to cool water.

- Hard, woody stems prefer to be conditioned in warm water.

- Rose stems cut diagonally at the bottom allow for maximum drinking opportunity, while placing them in warm water will encourage the blooms to open.

- Woody branches cut diagonally and crushed with a hammer at the tip will help them to uptake water.

- If hydrangeas wilt, discard excess leaves, as they zap energy needed for the blooms to thrive. Give them a fresh diagonal cut and transfer to fresh cold water in a clean vase. After a few hours, the head and blooms will become firm again.

- Never arrange daffodils with other flowers like tulips immediately after trimming the daffodil stems. Daffodils release a sap that will make other blooms wilt quickly. Condition daffodils in cool water for a few hours or overnight until they have released their fluids before moving on to arranging.

- A hot-water dip damages the stem's cells and allows them to uptake water more easily. This can be useful for soft-stemmed flowers, such as poppies, or to try to revive wilted blooms. When dipping, try to do so at an angle to avoid steaming the flowers.

- When euphorbia (also called spurge), poinsettias, or poppies are cut at a diagonal, they will release a milky sap. To stop this, dip the cut stem in hot water before continuing to use it in the arrangement.

- Cut hellebore stems in a lengthwise split from the first leaf to the bottom tip to allow for maximum water uptake.

- For flowers with hollow stems and heavy heads, such as hyacinths and amaryllis, insert straight off-cuts of rigid stems from fresh or wilted roses to provide supplemental support (see Love and Light arrangement, page 172). Alternatively, for flowers like ranunculus that have smaller stems, a single 18-gauge wire or wooden skewer can be inserted into the hollow stem, avoiding a poke through the flower head. Remove and rinse clean any wire for reuse before composting the spent flowers.

- Dramatic temperature changes can cause tulips to droop. When conditioning newly acquired bunches, leave them with their leaves intact wrapped in Kraft paper or newspaper for support. Leave them in tepid water at a moderate room temperature out of direct sun for at least 2 hours. Once they have adjusted to the temperature, remove the leaves before arranging.

- Each time I purchase peonies in bud, I can't help but wonder if they will ever open. They have almost always delivered, however, except for the few instances in which a waxlike accumulation of natural sugars has formed on the bud. If you notice this, lightly rinsing with tepid water helps to stimulate the flower. Gently squeezing the buds can also encourage the petals to reveal themselves.

Recycling Spent Flowers

In the last few years, a trend has emerged to use bleach to make flowers appear faded or antiqued. This look is considered a stunning feature by some and mimics the natural beauty of coveted and sometimes difficult-to-obtain cultivars such as 'La Belle Epoque' tulip. Some artists also spray-paint flowers to complete a certain design theme. Using these chemical alterations changes what is already offered by nature, and we forfeit the option to recycle them as compost that would otherwise cut greenhouse emissions. The use of compost provides numerous benefits, both directly through carbon sequestration and indirectly through improved soil health, reduced soil loss, increased water infiltration and storage, and reduction in other inputs. Whether composting your home arrangements or leftovers after a large event for a client, recycling chemical-free spent blooms can make a big impact on the health of our planet. If you cannot compost at home, look for local resources where you can donate your leftover or wilted flowers.

Rather than using dyed fresh flowers that cannot be composted, sugar flowers, such as the anemones used here, can capture the same look and feel but will last a lifetime.

CHAPTER EIGHT

Fresh and Sugar-Sweet Seasonal Arrangement Guides

The following compositions are examples of how to showcase any season's alluring possibilities of color, texture, and lavish petals with both drama and elegance. These tutorials are a workout for the eye, training you to see relationships in the vase and to acknowledge what resonates with your style. To achieve a natural rhythm as you work, avoid placing the base layer, focal flowers, or accents in a symmetrical manner. Acquire a varying number of stems to allow the arrangement to unfold with ease rather than adhering to a specific recipe. You may feel the arrangement is complete before you use them all, but you can feature these leftovers as single stems in multiple small bud vases, placed as playful accents alongside the arrangement or throughout a room. Although common flower names are used throughout, horticultural Latin names are provided when clarification is appropriate.

For each of the seasons, I provide one master class arrangement with complete and detailed step-by-step instructions and photos so that you can learn the process in depth, followed by two extra credit arrangements that you can use to further practice and hone your skills.

Adding something unexpected into a flower arrangement can transform the overall effect from beautifully pleasant to eye-catching and original. While there are often plenty of seasonal flowers and foliage available to achieve a fresh look, you can expand your palette of materials with another type of nature's gifts—flowers sculpted from sugar. Each season features one extra credit arrangement that shows you how to slip this surprising and unique feature into your work, drawing the eye in and begging the viewer to question its message.

Spring

Metamorphosis

I am frequently asked what my favorite flower is. This is impossible to answer, but whether real or sculpted in sugar, peonies have a dreamy presence that is easy to fall in love with. It is a dramatic flower that entertains throughout its entire bloom cycle, beginning as a small firm bud the size of a marble. As it unfurls in the most exquisite way, the flower increases tenfold, a miraculous spectacle to behold not unlike the remarkable transformation of a butterfly emerging from a cocoon. The larger and more ball-like, coral-apricot flowers of 'Coral Charm' peonies are often confused with the flatter, pinky-peach 'Coral Sunset' peonies. Although kindred spirits, 'Coral Charm' peonies are the stars of this arrangement, which begin unmistakably bright before elegantly fading to a pale ivory. This composition can easily be adapted to other showstoppers, such as roses or dahlias.

Equipment

Floral putty

Pin frog

Medium bowl-shaped vase

Chicken wire cushion (see page 125) (optional)

Cellophane tape (clear masking tape) (optional)

Turntable

Base Layer

3 large stems rose mallow (*Lavatera trimestris*)

3 soft pink dwarf hydrangea branches

Focal Flowers

30 stems coral peonies (*Paeonia* 'Coral Charm')

10 stems pale lavender to pink roses

Accent

5 stems blue milkweed (*Tweedia caerulea*)

Continued

1 Using a pinch of floral putty, secure the pin frog to the bottom of the bowl and fill it three-quarters full of cool-to-tepid water. If the bowl is very wide, place a chicken wire cushion on top of the pin frog and secure it to the rim of the vase with floral tape. Set the vase on a turntable. Cut three stems of the tree mallow into different lengths, keeping one stem long and the remaining lengths short. Position the tree mallow evenly throughout the vase with the longest stem secured in the frog on the left side for an asymmetrical feel.

2 The drama and elegance of peonies are given full attention in this arrangement when nestled among dainty mallow. Begin building the arrangement by cutting a few peonies to medium lengths and bending several over the rim. Stand a few tall stems and anchor them into the frog. As you work, create a cascading movement in the peony placement, directing the eye from the upper left corner to the bottom right side.

3 Continue building a robust base for the remaining peonies by placing the shortest hydrangeas only slightly above the rim. Cut five of the roses short and place them together with the hydrangea, securing both in the frog where possible. Place the remaining five roses in the arrangement, trimming as you go, in the same dynamic flow as the cascading peonies.

4 Hold any remaining peonies in the arrangement to consider if or how much they should be trimmed before their placement; the blooms should have ample room to breathe. To conclude, use the blue milkweed as filler throughout. Whimsical stems of the blue milkweed perform as a soft filler with playful color contrast.

Fleeting Moments

My sister-in-law Laura lives just a thirty-minute ride from Amsterdam in a picturesque town on the edge of a dike. Our family loves to visit in all seasons to ice-skate, swim, or sit in her beautiful summer garden. Every spring her massive lilac shrub comes into bloom with sturdy branches of deep purple and violet. Laura knows how much I love plants grown and gathered from a garden and always sends me back home with generous bunches of this fragrant flower gold.

There are fleeting moments in every season that must be fully embraced, or they are quickly lost for another year. Lilacs are certainly one of those. This moody arrangement displays the deep harmonious hues of the lilacs with blue and white columbine, clematis, and auriculas as delicate additions. Tulips in various shades of purple plus grape-purple roses enhance the majestic lilac ambiance. A small pin frog on a plate with water allows the auricula to be enjoyed with special attention to its rare and exquisite form.

Using a pinch of floral putty, secure a large pin frog to the bottom of a medium vase and fill it three-quarters full of water. Place a smaller pin frog on a small plate and set it aside. Divide one large lilac branch into smaller stems. Cut each stem at a diagonal or smash the thickest stems on the bottom with a hammer for maximum water intake. Discard excess bottom leaves, keeping a few above the water line to give the composition a fresh feel. Secure the lilacs in the frog with a few stems standing upright to form your base layer. Allow the heaviest blooms to spill over the rim and onto your table.

For the focal flowers, cut five grape-purple roses short and secure them into the pin frog among the lilac stems. Take twenty stems of mixed purple tulips (such as *Tulipa* 'Victoria's Secret', 'Blue Diamond', 'Blue Parrot', 'Slawa', and 'Affaire'), and before trimming them, look for stems that bend gracefully and set these aside. Cut the double flowering and parrot tulips short and tuck them evenly into the arrangement where they can be noticed. Place tulips with medium height upright in the remaining empty spaces, securing them in the frog where possible. To create some tension, allow the last tulips to elegantly bend and cross each other, creating an S-curve. Tuck two pale-pink to lavender clematis flowers (*Clematis* 'Darius') in between the tulips and lilacs on the right at the base of the composition.

To finish, trim ten stems of blue-purple and white bicolor columbine (*Aquilegia vulgaris*) to various lengths and scatter their playful bells throughout the arrangement as an accent. To evoke the feeling of a still life, secure two or three stems of dark purple auricula (*Primula auricula*) on the pin frog on the plate and set it next to the vase.

Reawakening

When spring finally arrives after the long gray months of winter, I can feel my mind and heart shifting. Although we may still experience cold snaps, ranunculus, anemone, daffodils, and tulips usher in the promise of warmer, brighter days. Yellow is the color we associate with the sun and is used here to visualize the light we so desperately crave. Daffodils are usually the first golden flowers to boldly peek above the ground, a true sign of relief!

When using tulips and daffodils in an arrangement with smaller blooms, after conditioning, remove as many of their leaves as possible to allow the full expression of their flowers. Tulips always grow taller in a vase—sometimes up to an inch a day. The seemingly whimsical bending of tulips is caused by the dual effects of continuing stem growth and the gentle pull of light and gravity (phototropism) on the flower head. A large blushing sugar rose inserted at the very end softens the bold yellows.

Begin by trimming fifteen stems of orange-trumpet, large cupped tazetta daffodils (*Narcissus* 'Johann Strauss' and 'Martinette') to different lengths and conditioning for at least a few hours, or up to overnight, to allow the sap to bleed (see page 129). Using a pinch of floral putty, secure a pin frog to the bottom of a footed, urn-shaped vase and fill it three-quarters full of cool-to-tepid water.

To create the base layer, separate two stems of white waxflower (*Chamelaucium* spp.) into multiple smaller stems. Loosely and evenly arrange them in the vase, securing the stems into the frog when possible. Cut twenty stems of mixed pink, bright pink-to-green, orange, and yellow ranunculus (also called Persian buttercups) (*Ranunculus* 'Elegance Cappuccino', 'Pon-Pon Malva', 'Clooney Lambada', and 'Success Omega') into different lengths. Tuck one fully open and stunning ranunculus on the front side of the arrangement, slightly above the rim. Reserving ample space on the right front side for the sugar rose, place the remaining ranunculus among the waxflowers. Position those with bent stems toward the edges, where they will explode forth like fireworks. Fill the remaining space with daffodils, working from the shortest stems in front to tallest in back.

Take twenty stems of yellow-edged apricot and red bicolor tulips (*Tulipa* 'Crossfire') and set aside six, two with the tallest stems and four with the shortest.

Cut the remaining fourteen tulips to various lengths and place throughout the arrangement, allowing their heads to arch with the weight of the petals and using them to fill empty spaces, with shorter stems at the rim and heavy flower heads falling gracefully from the sides. Place three stems of white windflower (*Anemone coronaria* 'Bride') on the left side so their flower centers resemble eyes searching for light. Pause to observe your display and insert three stems of burgundy and white or chartreuse bicolor carnations (*Dianthus caryophyllus*) to create accents of texture.

Lightly massage the stems of the two remaining long-stemmed tulips to help them bend naturally. Place one on the upper right, and another on the upper left. To change the tulip's familiar silhouette, use your thumb and index finger to gently flex the petals of the left tulip outward, making it appear as if it is a different flower. Add ten stems of small pale pink ranunculus (*Ranunculus* 'Elegance Pink Perfection') throughout to evoke lightness and place one blush Iceland poppy (*Papaver nudicaule*) as a focal point on the left. Gently place one large blush sugar rose (see page 206) on the bottom right side with its bloom turning downward, adjusting the wire if necessary.

To finish, place the four remaining yellow-edged apricot and 'Crossfire' tulips on the table near the vase to complete the composition.

Summer

Celebrating Abundance

The shoulder season between spring and summer is when flowers enjoy the accelerating momentum of warmth while taking the last breath of cool, wet days. Combining the best of both worlds by using peonies, roses, lupines, and poppies together creates a joyful celebration of this abundant time. Densely arched or recurved branches of ninebark are the base layer that give structure and strength to the composition, while lady's mantle and butterfly weed give extra support and cushion to the 'Vuvuzela' roses. These dramatic flowers are the stars of the arrangement and will speak to you with different voices. Allow their dialogue to unfold in the vase with a cheerful cadence that honors their unique attributes. I prefer 'Coral Sunset' and 'Sarah Bernhardt' peonies as a contrast to the dark ninebark foliage, but you should choose the cultivars that captivate you or are available in a similar color spectrum. The Russell hybrid lupines are commonly found in the trade and provide substantial, often erect or stiff stems, but they may also curve in animated ways that provide a gesture of drama. Select one medium globe allium and, with careful placement, invite consideration of its elegantly long stem. Carnations—often undeservingly considered mundane—elevate their floral companions with their frilly ruffled petals. Cornflowers and drumstick allium are exclamation marks that finish and lighten the composition.

Equipment

Floral putty

Pin frog

Tall flared vase

Base Layer

2 or 3 ninebark branches (*Physocarpus opulifolius*)

7 to 9 stems butterfly weed (*Asclepius tuberosa*)

5 to 7 stems lady's mantle (*Alchemilla mollis*)

6 to 8 coral-blush to pink garden roses (*Rosa* 'Vuvuzela')

Focal Flowers

3 stems coral peonies (*Paeonia* 'Coral Sunset')

3 stems blush or pink peonies (*Paeonia* 'Sarah Bernhardt')

3 to 5 stems pink or purple garden lupines (*Lupinus polyphyllus*)

3 to 6 stems peach carnations (*Dianthus caryophyllus*)

3 stems wine-red poppies (*Papaver* spp.)

1 stem medium globe allium (*Allium hollandicum* 'Purple Sensation')

Accents

1 to 3 stems drumstick allium (*Allium sphaerocephalon*)

3 stems pink to red cornflowers or bachelor buttons (*Centaurea cyanus*)

Continued

1 Using a pinch of floral putty, secure a pin frog to the bottom of your vase and fill it three-quarters full of cool-to-tepid water. Trim the ninebark stems to different lengths and anchor them into the frog, creating an asymmetrical but supportive base layer.

2 Position the butterfly weed, trimmed in different lengths, as a cushion for the base flowers and focal flowers. Add the lady's mantle, cut relatively short, among and throughout the butterfly weed. Its chartreuse pop will add a fresh brightness to the robust blooms that follow. Loosely fill out the center with the roses.

3 Cut the peonies into various lengths. When nestling them into the vase, note how their presence commands attention with an upward motion and gives a sense of flair when facing outward, or allows the heart to rest when bending in repose.

4 Cut the lupines in various lengths and place them where they add a sense of drama, curling into or swooping away from the arrangement. Add carnations to amplify the abundance, and delicately snuggle the fragile poppies throughout. If the globe allium appears stiff, carefully massage the stem and, without force, gently bend it to achieve a graceful curve. Position it as a subtle distraction and to add some intrigue. To finish, use the whimsical drumstick allium and cornflowers as playful accents or fillers.

Chasing the Sun

The heads of sunflowers tend to twist throughout the day as they follow the sun's lead, a circadian rhythm that humans also share. The sizable blooms and cheerful faces of 'Tiger's Eye' sunflowers have wide-reaching petals that echo the rays of the sun and bring the warmth of the season indoors. Their internal clock provides inspiration for this impressive hallway arrangement that blesses our family when we leave and welcomes us back home. Our entrance is always a colder temperature, especially in summer, and this prolongs the longevity of the arrangement.

If there is one flower that is reliably generous, it is the hydrangea. One stem is comprised of a multitude of playful little florets that hold their form in gardens and pots all season long. If we are lucky, they linger well into autumn, changing to softer tones from their summer selves. When we use foliage as a base layer, the abundance of hydrangea florets and color provides a head start for building a generous display.

Using a pinch of floral putty, secure a pin frog to the bottom of a sizable tall vase with a wide opening and fill it three-quarters full of water. Begin creating the base layer by anchoring two stems of soft to bright pink tree mallow (*Malva arborea*) into the frog toward the left side with room to reveal their delicate flowers. Trim the remaining three stems to different lengths and place throughout the vase. Trim four blue mophead hydrangea branches (*Hydrangea macrophylla*) and position them between the mallow: the first stem on the left, the second on the right spilling over the rim, a third in the middle, and the final in the back loosely over the rim. Position three white mophead or smooth hydrangea branches (*Hydrangea macrophylla* or *H. arborescens*) on the outside to dance over the front and side-facing rim.

Set aside three of twelve stems sunflower (*Helianthus annuus* 'Tiger's Eye') and trim the rest to medium lengths. Nestle the shortest stems on the outside of the arrangement tucked in between the base layer, and the slightly taller stems in the middle of the arrangement. If you are unsure about a suitable length, keep them long and hold them in the arrangement to test the trim size.

Cut ten stems of soft pink roses into different lengths, keeping the stems that elegantly bend with more length. Feed them into any empty spaces with room to unfurl or allow them to naturally spill out of the arrangement as if draping over a fence. Take the time to consider where the longest rose will attract the most attention and place it accordingly. Crown the arrangement with one long sunflower positioned toward the light to simulate its natural growth. Add three stems blue milkweed (*Tweedia caerulea*) and three stems of lily of the Nile (*Agapanthus africanus*) as finishing accents of airy coolness that calm the brightness of summer.

A Wild Meadow

Summer is the perfect time to experiment with boldness. The flower choices can be overwhelming when there is so much available, but why pick a color scheme? Focus instead on building tones, textures, and shapes to give this arrangement depth and welcome joy without restraint. Chartreuse 'Green Jewel' coneflower adds freshness and light while white Japanese anemones provide rest in between a riot of colors. A soft pink sugar rose becomes a focal point that gives nuance and balance to a wild meadow–inspired mood.

Using a pinch of floral putty, secure a pin frog to the bottom of a medium vase and fill it three-quarters full of cool-to-tepid water. Set the vase on a turntable to assist with arranging. Cut a few side stems from the bottom of four generous branches of soft pink rose mallow (*Malva* spp.) and place the side stems loosely in the vase to form an evenly spaced base layer framework. Keep the remaining branches of the mallow to fill out a towering arrangement. Four white panicle hydrangea branches (*Hydrangea paniculata*) perform as a blank canvas and are the perfect base layer for the rainbow of bloom colors in this arrangement. Keep one long stem and trim the remaining three branches into different lengths. Anchor them all into the pin frog, with one long stem on the left and the others falling over the rim to the right and back side of the arrangement. Lightly trim the remaining mallow branches and secure them into the frog among the hydrangeas. Rotate the turntable and make sure your base layer is evenly secured in the vase.

Cut seven stems of yellow roses into different lengths. Place the roses with softly bent stems along the outside rim of the vase so they spill over in a playful way. Continue dispersing the remaining roses evenly throughout the arrangement. Trim one orange rose to a medium length and position it where it will be fully appreciated and make the strongest impression. Cut five green coneflowers (*Echinacea* 'Green Jewel') into different lengths and scatter throughout. Use six California lilac sprigs (*Ceanothus* spp.) to fill in any open spaces. Gently nudge some flowers aside and nestle one pink mum prominently in the middle. Place one burgundy dahlia at the rim where it will arch over gracefully.

Continue by trimming about seven stems of burgundy and eight stems of purple cosmos flowers into different lengths. Position a few along the rim and some toward the crown, allowing their flower heads to dance exuberantly over the others. Place three white Japanese anemones (*Eriocapitella japonica* syn. *Anemone hupehensis*) where the arrangement could use some highlights. To finish, carefully place a soft pink sugar rose (see page 206) toward the bottom center, so it is quietly noticeable.

Fall

The Last Splash

Despite our obsession with the fervor of youth, autumn reminds us that it is both natural and magnificent for a verdant landscape to transition into dormancy and eventual decay. Before leaves blanket the ground with the last splash of gold and petals are singed with frost, we are beckoned to a convivial party of color and texture. Oak leaves that display a transitional range of color from green and leathery brown to crimson-tipped bronze provide the backbone of this overflowing composition. Forage the branches if possible, including additional hydrangea, if necessary, and combine what unique leaves you can find with velvety amaranth in warm tones of burgundy and gold. Plump crabapples offer height and drip from the edges of the vase with glowing cherry-size fruit. Big full dahlias and bright chrysanthemums offer a splendid finale before turning inward for winter. This tribute to the glowing forests of autumn is a warm consolation for saying goodbye to the carefree days of summer. The conclusion is a generous and overflowing display, but as always, feel free to stop when the composition pleases you.

Equipment

Floral putty

Pin frog

Generous V-shaped vase

Chicken wire cushion (see page 125)

Cellophane tape (clear masking tape)

Base Layer

8 oak branches (*Quercus* spp.)

10 stems burgundy amaranth (*Amaranthus cruentus* 'Burgundy Glow')

10 stems golden amaranth (*Amaranthus cruentus* 'Hot Biscuit')

4 crabapple branches (*Malus* spp.)

Focal Flowers

12 stems gold and red mums (*Chrysanthemum* spp.)

8 stems yellow yarrow (*Achillea* spp.)

18 stems apricot, salmon, and orange and yellow bicolor dahlias (*Dahlia* spp.)

Accents

2 to 3 stems Chinese lanterns (*Alkekengi officinarum* syn. *Physalis alkekengi*)

1 rosehip branch (*Rosa multiflora*)

5 stems Chinese bittersweet (*Celastrus orbiculatus*)

Continued

1 Using a pinch of floral putty, secure a pin frog to the bottom of your vase and place the chicken wire cushion on top. Secure the cushion with cellophane tape (clear masking tape) and fill the vase three-quarters full of cool-to-tepid water. Cut the oak branches to different lengths. Secure the longest branch into the frog, slightly off from the middle, so that it demands attention. Position the remaining stems into the frog, avoiding symmetry as you proceed. Cut the amaranth into various lengths and place them as dance partners to the oak leaves, following their lead.

2 The dainty red berries of crabapple expand the palette of warmth and bring in a fresh element of movement to the composition. Secure three branches into the frog so they gracefully bend over the rim and relax onto the table with the weight of their fruits. Place one branch upright and to one side so that the fruit dangles airily.

A kaleidoscope of dahlias and mums in energizing tones fills out the arrangement, along with yellow yarrow to provide cushioning where necessary. Cut the mums into different lengths and secure one long stem along the rising length of the crabapple. Place the yarrow where the arrangement could use some extra cushioning and to eliminate any dark or empty spaces.

3 Cut the dahlias into different lengths and position them in relationship to the mums. Be sure that some playfully poke out of the arrangement in a hide-and-seek reveal of their perfectly rounded heads.

4 Plump and novel Chinese lanterns are a welcome contrast to the lush textures of the focal flowers and amplify their character. Use one or two stems to spill over the rim of the vase and float onto the table. Nestle another into the arrangement standing upright. Now take a step back to observe the composition, noting the rhythm of the flowers and branches. Place the rosehip branch where you feel the arrangement could benefit from some extra drama. Finally, position a few stems of Chinese bittersweet at the rim of the vase, reserving the tallest stem for a preeminent role that surpasses the height of all other stems.

The Comeback of the Chrysanthemum

The ancient chrysanthemum (or mum) has long been considered a relic of the past—prompting memories of stiff stems and anything but elegant beauty. They carry a regretful and undeserved reputation for being old-fashioned, but today's mums are not what they used to be. Once-unfashionable flowers are now trending as more graceful versions of themselves, and thankfully, mums are making such a comeback. Breeders are developing new cultivars or reintroducing heirloom types with lithe stems and feathery, spooned, or quilled petals. No longer rigid and fussy, these complex dignified flowers are rivaling their showy autumn counterparts like the beloved dahlia.

The name "chrysanthemum" originates from the Greek words *chrysos* (precious things made of gold) and *anthemon* (flower), confirming that they are indeed flower gold! Despite their lustrous qualities, they are often less expensive compared with other flowers and offer a lot of va-va-voom for your money, especially in the ever-expanding world of competitive new introductions. If you want to splurge, however, buy single stems of rare large-flowered mums whose specialized care and months of precise pinching, staking, and grooming will certainly cost you a fortune. Whatever selections find their way into your hands, mums promise an incredibly long vase life, especially if you change or top off the water regularly, and they will reward your purchase with plenty of flower power.

Golden chrysanthemums, burgundy dahlias, and 'Miss Piggy' roses with a sugar rose and sugar anemones dispersed throughout (see pages 206 and 212) for contrast and romance.

Floral Renaissance

There are so many new varieties of mums that each year, it is nearly impossible to choose which colors and forms to display in my home. Mums are truly the harbinger of autumn, arriving just as roses and dahlias begin waning in the nippy air. This is the time to embrace flowers that push beyond the typical warm sunset colors of this season. One of my favorite combinations is to pair exotic spider mums with softer tones of blush, pink, and lavender. This composition uses a considerable number of stems, but the feeling they evoke can also be achieved with fewer. As a bonus, reuse the Chinese bittersweet branches in dried arrangements long after your fresh roses and mums have withered.

Using a pinch of floral putty, secure a pin frog to the bottom of a large vase and fill it three-quarters full of cool-to-tepid water. Select forty to forty-five stems of mixed pink, peach, copper, and lavender mums (about four bunches) and set aside a few with unique character to finish the arrangement. Their lively movement will end any preconceived notions of stodginess.

Sturdy hydrangea branches with a few leaves left above the water line offer structure for the other flowers. To create the base layer, cut three stems of lime mophead or smooth hydrangea branches (*Hydrangea macrophylla* or *H. arborescens*) into various lengths with their flower heads sitting slightly above the rim of the vase and anchor them into the frog. Cut four stems of euphorbia (*Euphorbia fulgens* 'Sunstream') into different lengths and dip each into hot water for 5 to 10 seconds to stop the milky sap from bleeding. Use them to fill out the base layer and establish support for the heavier mums.

Cut the mums into different lengths as you fill out the arrangement. Begin with the shorter stems, and working from the outside in, build a cadence by adding longer stems and avoiding symmetry.

Cut seven stems of blush roses into different lengths and snuggle them in where the arrangement can use extra contrast, cushioning, or focus. Take a step back to note how the conversation is developing between the stems and finish with the mums that were set aside earlier. Bend a few playfully over the rim of the vase, while placing others standing tall to create movement. Give one stem of cheery 'Inga' mum with a yellow daisy-like center prominent placement as a resting place for the eye to settle.

Secure some hooks or nails into the wall behind the arrangement. Tie small loops of thread around the ends of five stems of Chinese bittersweet (*Celastrus orbiculatus*) and hang them, allowing their swooping forms to dangle wildly, adding texture and drama to the scene. Shorten any remaining mums or roses with outstanding features and fill complementary bud vases to create an autumn vignette. To finish, scatter dried leaves and hydrangea blossoms along the foreground of your stunning arrangement.

Summer Farewell

When autumn arrives with shimmering gold and copper leaves, yellow and orange sneezeweed become the perfect companions to the last offering of pink and apricot late summer roses. Sugar flowers make a subtle but bold statement of floral pleasure that defies preconceived boundaries of the seasons. Enjoy this arrangement as a subtle farewell to the sweet days of summer and a warm welcome to tea and cake by the fireplace.

Using a pinch of floral putty, secure a pin frog to the bottom of a footed, urn-shaped vase and place a chicken wire cushion (page 125) on top. Secure the cushion with cellophane tape (clear masking tape) and fill the vase three-quarters full of cool-to-tepid water.

To create the base layer, anchor three of five stems of sneezeweed (*Helenium autumnale*) into the pin frog before positioning four tall stems of Chinese bittersweet (*Celastrus orbiculatus*) branches cut to different lengths. Feature the versatility of Chinese bittersweet by standing one curved stem tall in the vase and the remaining three branches in a dangling repose over the edge. Select ten stems each of pink and peach long-stemmed roses and set aside two of each color that have a beguiling bend. Position one fully open rose in the front, one on the side, and one in the back resting slightly over the rim of the vase. Fill the vase with the remaining roses and eight stems of soft pink dahlias trimmed to various lengths. Take a step back and identify empty spaces before placing three of the longer bent rose stems throughout. Position the last and tallest rose slightly in the middle to command attention.

Cut four stems of pink cosmos (*Cosmos bipinnatus*) into different lengths and add along with six California lilac branches (*Ceanothus* spp.) and five stems of golden amaranth (*Amaranthus*

cruentus 'Hot Biscuit') for asymmetrical playfulness throughout. Accents of ten bright and fiery red-orange falling stars (also called montbretia) (*Crocosmia aurea*) give this arrangement some added light, timed appropriately for the shortening days. Separate the two remaining stems of sneezeweed into single flowers and intersperse their cheerfulness throughout. Trail one (8- to 12-inch) piece of cascading pale to medium-blue clematis vine (*Clematis* spp.) along a stem of Chinese bittersweet, allowing its cool blue to complement the warm autumnal tones and add extra drama.

To hold on to summer for one last moment, gently nudge aside a few roses. Carefully place a sugar peony (see page 198) at the base of the arrangement, resting softly in between the cushion of roses and elegantly bending over the rim of the vase. Give focus to the sugar flower by carefully bending its wire as necessary. For a subtle surprise, slip a sugar anemone (see page 212) into the arrangement as another sneaky gesture of seasonal defiance. Arrange apples, pomegranates, or any real fruits and a variety of sugar flowers on the table around the vase to complete the still-life atmosphere and provide days of delightful decor.

Winter

Romance

Almost 24,000 acres of Dutch greenhouses come to the rescue well before and long after flowers and vegetables are officially in season. Thankfully, the latest solar and water recycling technology and increased use of organic cultivation are continuously advancing these growers toward climate-neutral operations. From seedling to packaging, these automated greenhouses are like floral theme parks, with blooms riding on roller-coaster conveyor belts all the way to their boxes. It is a true spectacle of ingenuity and innovation, and I am forever grateful for the winter flower gold they provide.

Multiple studies have shown that the presence of flowers, more than any other item of pleasure, can indeed change one's state of mind. When the choice is between gray skies or Dutch-grown winter roses, I will joyfully choose the latter any day. Roses are my favorite greenhouse-grown flower to fight the winter blues, and they are increasingly available in fragrant options. Although they are most often supporting characters in my work, this arrangement shifts the focus to their romantic allure, which is elevated by a cake pedestal. Choose a selection that appeals to you with variations of color and striking forms including singles, doubles, and spray roses. Although fragrance is not common in greenhouse-grown roses, search for them and splurge if you can!

Equipment

Floral putty

Pin frog

Medium bowl

Chicken wire cushion
(see page 125)

Cellophane tape (clear
masking tape)

Sturdy cake stand or
pedestal

Base Layer

10 stems lady's mantle
(*Alchemilla mollis*)

Focal Flowers

30 stems assorted
double-flowered,
single-flowered, and
spray roses (about
3 bunches) in white,
buttercream, blush,
pink, lavender, yellow,
apricot, or any other
pastel colors

Continued

1 Using a pinch of floral putty, secure a pin frog to the bottom of your bowl and place the chicken wire cushion on top. Secure the cushion with cellophane tape (clear masking tape) and fill the vase three-quarters full of cool-to-tepid water.

2 The bright and fresh pop of chartreuse lady's mantle performs as a soft and luminescent shelter for the roses. Divide the lady's mantle, keeping a few stems long. Gently push the delicate stems into the frog, dangling the longest ones loosely over the edge.

3 Trim a favorite double-flowered rose short, rest it over the edge, and secure the stem into the pin frog. Keep one stem of spray roses long and secure it into the upper left of the arrangement. Trim another stem of spray roses short and position it in the middle to provide volume and lightness.

4 Trim some of the single roses into different lengths and stand one long stem in the upper right corner. Use the others to fill the center and sides, dangling any bent stems over the rim. If stems of lady's mantle become buried while placing the roses, give them a gentle tug to encourage their reappearance. Before continuing further, take a pause to examine if all the roses are secured firmly into the pin frog and observe whether the composition is to your liking. Continue trimming and tucking the remaining roses into empty spaces, varying their placement in height and color. When almost finished, place the bowl on a pedestal/cake stand to see if the arrangement meets your expectation. Relish each fragrant rose with consideration and joy!

Love and Light

When daylight shortens, we celebrate holiday traditions with festive evergreens, winter blooms, and twinkling candles whose light reflects from a crystal vase. Mistletoe hung from the ceiling is a welcome excuse to offer a kiss to those we cherish. This celebrated sprig, a token of love, is also the perfect base layer to any arrangement. The alluring balm of eucalyptus together with the heavenly scent of the tuberose and roses fills the home with lasting fragrance, allowing us to experience their presence with all our senses. Amaryllis that begins as a tight bud emerges with confidence and determination, pushing ever upward before exploding with a splash of crimson. It is an entertaining spectacle that can last for up to two weeks. Cut amaryllis stems short and arrange them in a small vase to bring attention to their wondrous nature.

I never miss an opportunity to include hellebores in winter arrangements and have planted a generous amount on my rooftop so I can snip at will. Peruvian lilies (*Alstroemeria* spp.) are workhorses with blooms thriving for days. Sensual still-life display fruits complement the holiday atmosphere of aromatic pies roasting in the oven and glittering salads adorned with pomegranate jewels.

Using a pinch of floral putty, secure a pin frog to the bottom of a crystal-footed vase and fill it three-quarters full of cool-to-tepid water. Set the vase on a turntable to assist with arranging all sides. Cut small branches from three stems of mistletoe (*Viscum album*) and one large blue gum eucalyptus branch (*Eucalyptus globulus*) and anchor them into the frog with their leaves spilling over the edge. Set aside one or two longer pieces of curved eucalyptus.

Set aside five to seven elegant stems of thirty assorted lavender, apricot, and yellow-orange roses and trim the twenty-three to twenty-five remaining roses short. Keep a few rose stem trimmings for later use. Fill the vase with roses to create a slightly domed shape, working from the outside in and alternating with different colors and varieties. Cut three stems of red and white bicolor amaryllis (*Hippeastrum* spp.) to a preferable length. Remove any thorns from the saved rose trimmings if you haven't already and fill the hollow stem of the amaryllis with the saved rose stem for support. Tuck the amaryllis into a space on the right about

the same height as the roses. Rotate your turntable and repeat this step of filling another hollow amaryllis stem with a rose stem and place it on the backside of the arrangement.

Place the longer roses to casually flow from the arrangement. Add seven stems of tuberose (*Agave amica* syn. *Polianthes tuberosa*) cut to different lengths for strokes of light and texture. Gently place three stems of Christmas rose (*Helleborus niger*) or Lenten rose (*Helleborus orientalis*) in the arrangement to lighten any dark cavities. Repeat this step with three stems of dark pink and white bicolor Peruvian lily (*Alstroemeria* spp.).

To finish with a still-life ambiance, place eight to ten pieces of fresh fruit (figs, apples, pomegranates, and so on) in a bowl at the foot of the vase. Cut an amaryllis short and rest its heavy bloom on the rim of a bud vase. Light some candles and enjoy an intimate moment with a glass of *glühwein*!

Garden Fantasy

Garden-grown flowers are scarce during late winter, and we must be resourceful when building arrangements that are colorful and abundant. When the days lengthen, the first branches of lilacs, fragrant viburnum, and apple blossoms make a much-anticipated return to the markets. They beautifully support greenhouse-grown roses, ranunculus, and tulips, a reliable trio of flowers that play in harmony with the tune of any season. Sometimes I envision this arrangement as a fantasy garden on the cusp of early summer, dividing it into sections that reflect how the plants would naturally grow. Some stems are trimmed short, while others remain long, a natural consequence of their different responses to light and warmth. Seeking refuge in everlasting sugar flowers is the perfect finish to this soft dreamscape, especially with accent flowers that resemble delphiniums made with blue flower paste, using the sugar cherry blossom method (see page 224).

Using a pinch of floral putty, secure a pin frog to the bottom of a medium vase and place a chicken wire cushion (see page 125) on top. Secure the cushion with cellophane tape (clear masking tape) and fill the vase three-quarters full of cool-to-tepid water. Trim five laurustinus branches (*Viburnum tinus*) short and secure them in the pin frog to begin creating a balanced base layer, discarding any leaves that meet the water. Trim ten lilac branches (*Syringa vulgaris*) to medium lengths and stand some upright in the pin frog while dangling the heavy flower clusters of others loosely over the rim. Finish the base layer with three European cranberry viburnum branches (*Viburnum opulus*) by positioning a taller stem in between the lilac and laurustinus and place another opposite on the bottom right, allowing its heavy snowball head to relax onto the table.

Trim four stems of pale lavender and apricot roses short and add them evenly throughout, making sure to rest two in the front in between the lilacs. Cut a few of the twenty stems of cerise and orange ranunculus (*Ranunculus* 'Elegance Cerise' and *R. asiaticus* 'Elegance Orange') short and place them along the front rim of the vase. Leave the other ranunculus stems long and find room for them in the center. Remove most of the leaves from six of seven stems of apricot parrot tulips, five double lilac tulips, and four pink fringed tulips. Trim the

stems short and use them to fill any empty spaces. Use any remaining long-stemmed tulips to spill out of the arrangement, pausing to observe their impact. Nestle three of four short-stemmed peach carnations (*Dianthus caryophyllus* 'Antigua') snugly in between the other flowers' space and place one long-stemmed carnation on the upper right to balance out the composition.

Tuck one white camellia into the bottom right to enhance the cascading movement of the arrangement. Use three or four branches of apple blossoms as exclamation marks in the back and two shorter stems of flowering dill (*Anethum graveolens*) for lightness throughout. Place one taller stem of flowering dill on the right as a companion to the tulip and carnation. Position a sugar rose (see page 206) right in the middle and gently make room for a sugar tulip (see page 218) on the right above the camellia. If it is necessary to increase the height of the sugar flowers, tape an 18-gauge wire to the stems or insert the sharp wire of the sugar flower into a leftover rose stem, pushing it in a few inches to firmly secure. Once increased in length, trim if necessary. Carefully place one stem of a blue accent flower (use the sugar cherry blossoms method on page 224, but with blue flower paste) for a sweet final touch.

PART V

Sweet Moments

Creating a "sweet garden" of sugar flowers is an opportunity to enhance every day and celebratory moments with these distinctive treasures. Sugar flowers can be used in fresh floral arrangements with the dexterity of the Dutch Masters who were some of the first to manipulate seasonal flower combinations in an expression of fantasy. Sugar flowers can also bring an air of elegant festivity, especially when used to adorn cakes for weddings, anniversaries, and themed parties. Use my simple vanilla sponge recipe to cover with buttercream and fondant as an edible canvas for sugar flowers. Constructing and decorating these cakes is simple, and my straightforward tutorial will assist you with the timing and storage of the cake along with preservation considerations of sugar flowers for a lifetime of memories.

The possibilities of sugar flowers are limitless, but we must begin somewhere. The peony, garden rose, anemone, tulip, and cherry blossom are starting points for developing the skills necessary to explore this versatile medium. Try to appreciate the essence of each flower petal or pistil as you sculpt them one by one.

I feel obligated to warn you that sculpting sugar flowers is extremely addictive, especially once you become more comfortable with the process! With some practice, looking at fresh blossoms will never be the same. Observing the structure of petals, the texture of leaves, and the intricate reproductive flower centers creates a deep awareness of their biology. This activity is relaxing and meditative and has the potential to change the way you experience and interact with plants. With each sugar flower that you make, observe how your placement of it in an arrangement or on a cake has changed with the new intimacy that you have developed. The result is a paradigm shift in thinking that can be challenging in the beginning but, above all, is extremely rewarding.

CHAPTER NINE

Creating a Sweet Garden

My flower paste recipe and techniques have been tested and tweaked to sculpt fleeting moments of detail with ease. It is adaptable to European and North American ingredients and creates a malleable paste that hardens into an heirloom relic of time and place. Creating sugar flowers can be broken down into steps to allow easy replication of the stamens, pistils, petals, buds, and leaves. Beginning with multi-petaled flowers such as the peony may seem excessive, but it encourages the repetition necessary to become comfortable with using flower paste. Regardless of what flower you choose to create first, a few essential tools are necessary to assemble. Read through the basics at least once to familiarize yourself with the tools and ingredients and to discover tips for success. Once you have an idea of the process, you can divide it into stages that accommodate your free time, including time for creating and resting the paste, coloring the paste, creating and drying the centers of the flowers, and making and assembling the petals into a finished flower.

Re-creating nature's wonders in sugar may seem intimidating at first. But once you embark upon this journey, it will quickly become a very rewarding activity for many reasons. Creating sugar flowers can be considered a gift to yourself by setting aside the time to focus and offer attention to the process. When we let go of expectations and mental clutter, we also remove a lot of stress and anxiety that may otherwise hinder our flow. It takes consistent work to set these intentions and eliminate unnecessary distractions from our lives, but it is worth it.

When getting started with sugar flowers, reserve four to eight hours of uninterrupted time to explore and become comfortable with your tools and the medium. Designate a small area to get started where your tools do not have to be cleared for the day, especially if you take a break. If you do not have a desk, a corner of your kitchen countertop will suffice. Turn off your phone, pour a cup of warm tea, and relax into the study of your chosen flower specimen.

Practice and patience are all you need to become a sugar flower artist. If moments of doubt creep in, trust yourself and ask: What is the worst that can really happen? Although the flowers in the forthcoming pages strive to emulate nature's flawless beauty, it is important to remember there is no such thing as perfection. Inconsistencies are what make life so interesting and these creations so special. Be gentle with yourself as you learn and relish in the discoveries you make that customize the process to match your aesthetic. Be bold when using color, experiment with different cutters, or use extra force

with your CelPin or ball tool; it's the success of these experiments that will encourage you to take risks and enjoy the surprising rewards. I still look forward to those accidental creative moments that deepen my work.

The Essential Sugar Flower Tool Kit

When I began making sugar flowers, I spent needless money on unnecessary tools. The following is a basic and relatively inexpensive kit whose components can be purchased online for creating, modeling, and coloring flower paste (see Resources, page 238). In addition to these fundamental items, each sugar flower project requires a few more specialized tools. These are listed under the equipment list for each sugar flower and are necessary to create nuanced details that bring life to the peony, garden rose, anemone, tulip, and cherry blossom.

Although color theory and the color wheel do not guide my flower arranging process, creating depth of color in sugar flowers requires a thoughtful eye and a robust color kit that you can build and add to over time. Included here are some basic items you will need for coloring flower centers and petals. When purchasing liquid gel color, petal dusts, and pollen, remember that blending is key to achieving a realistic result. For specific recommendations of liquid gel colors and petal dusts for coloring flower paste, see the equipment list for each sugar flower project.

Flower Model

Each phase in the life of a flower has the potential to inspire, from the bud to a full bloom, to the moments of wilt and decay. Study these and be encouraged to re-create each as a tribute to their fleeting existence. Cultivating joy in creating is key here—allow artistic freedom and be surprised by what follows. Fresh blossoms will always triumph in appeal, but trying to get as close to the original using sugar is thrilling. Wabi-sabi, the Japanese art of accepting transience, can be applied to sugar work and help you to embrace imperfections. Accidental holes in a petal or a tear in a leaf give interest and character to a sugar flower. Don't immediately reject work that isn't considered perfect.

Choose a bloom that inspires you and place it in a vase by your table. As you work, notice the petal texture, colors, movement, and overall botanical appearance and size. If you are creating a flower out of season, the internet, botanical illustrations, or books with photographs of beautiful flowers (see Resources, page 238) can be helpful resources for gathering images as substitutes for the real thing.

Liquid egg whites

Liquid egg whites, which can be found in the refrigerated section of the grocery store, near the eggs, are used as an adhesive, but be careful not to use too much. Excess egg white will make the flower paste sticky and prevent petal dust from adhering. I use the side of my nondominant hand to wipe away excess from wires, but paper towels work as well. Avoid flower paste "swimming" in egg white at all times.

Cornstarch with cornstarch dusting pouch

Cornstarch can be used to dip your fingers in while working or to dust a work surface to prevent flower paste from sticking. Store it in a cornstarch dusting pouch that can be purchased online or from a craft store, created specifically for sugar flower making to prevent it from becoming messy.

Vegetable shortening

Vegetable shortening is useful for adjusting the pliability of flower paste. If the paste begins to feel dry while you are working, massage pea-size amounts of shortening into the paste until it becomes soft and smooth.

Wire cutter

This tool cuts floral wires of gauges 18 to 33 into halves, thirds, quarters, or smaller if needed.

Needle-nose pliers

This tool bends the end of wires into hooks that are needed for attaching to flower paste. These pliers are also helpful for inserting sugar flowers into a cake.

Embroidery scissor set

These razor-sharp scissors have superfine ends that are more precise than regular household scissors. They often come as a set and are useful for creating texture for the small, detailed parts of sugar flowers such as the peony, rose, and anemone.

9-inch rolling pin

This size rolling pin is perfect for the initial rolling of flower paste onto a groove board.

6-inch long and ¾-inch wide nonstick polyethylene rolling pin (medium CelCakes Brand CelPin)

This rolling pin is smaller than a 9-inch rolling pin, allowing greater dexterity, especially when working with small amounts of flower paste. It is used to roll and thin out the sugar petals after they have been cut to increase their size and make them appear more natural. Take this into consideration when choosing the size of a petal cutter. The light, nonstick material and size of the CelCakes Medium CelPin is my preferred brand for achieving my desired results. It can also be used as a substitute for a ball tool.

Floral wire, gauges 18 to 33

Floral wire comes in different thicknesses ranging from 16-gauge to 33-gauge. The lower the gauge number, the thicker the wire.

FMM Dresden tool (flute and vein tool)

This tool has two sides: a wide end and a thin and elongated pointed end used to add definition and for modeling petals and pistils. It is a great tool to create cavities or a mark in pistils, to curl sugar petals along the edges, and to create veins in leaves. The FMM brand Dresden tool has the perfect size width on both ends that is especially helpful for creating the peony, anemone, and tulip.

Flower foam pad

This pad is specifically designed for sugar craft and provides a stable, nonstick work surface with the necessary firmness and bounce to allow you to create and model naturally shaped sugar petals, leaves, and flowers.

Nonstick groove board, with smooth reverse side

A nonstick groove board, also called a veining board, has dual functionality. The groove creates a middle vein when rolling out flower paste that is

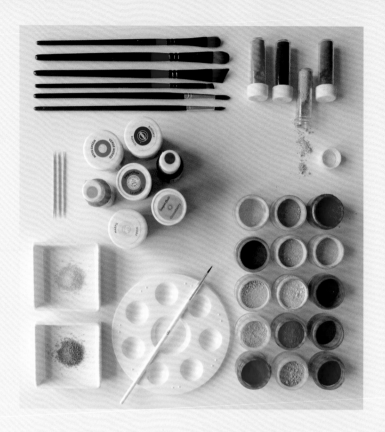

for inserting wires into petals and leaves with ease. The groove board can be flipped for a smooth work surface that is indispensable when creating sugar flowers.

Styropor cake dummy or a block of Styrofoam, at least 4 by 4 inches

Styrofoam has many uses, including to dry flower centers, to stage flowers for observing and adjusting their posture, or to visualize how sugar flowers will look on a cake.

Hamilworth floral tapes, green, in ½-inch and ¼-inch widths

Floral tape is used to assemble the various parts of sugar flowers and to finish floral wires. The brand Hamilworth manufactures ½-inch (whole) and ¼-inch (half width) tape in the largest variety of colors (I mostly use "Nile Green"). Stretch the tape to release its glue and wrap it around the wire of a sugar flower to create a lifelike stem. To make half-width tape yourself, wrap full-width tape a few times around three fingers. Flatten the circle of tape and cut it in half lengthwise with scissors.

Paintbrushes, various sizes

Use soft brushes in different sizes and tips (round and flat) to apply petal dust to individual petals and finished flowers. Brushes with fine round ends apply liquid egg white with precision.

These should not be expensive brushes, but using ones with short hair won't absorb more dust than necessary and avoids waste. Wash your brushes in lukewarm water with a little bit of soap.

Toothpicks

These are used to easily and cleanly transfer small amounts of liquid gel colors to flower paste, preventing unnecessary waste.

Petal dusts, various colors

Petal dust comes in a large selection of colors and can be edible or not. Always check the packaging and match it to your intended use. Various brands carry different colors with tempting names (see Resources, page 238). Build your collection as you become more experienced, but there are many different personalized shades you can achieve by mixing just a few basic colors together on a sheet of white parchment paper.

Liquid gel colors, various colors

Various brands carry edible liquid gel colors that can be used in small amounts to color flower paste.

Painter's palette

Ideal for mixing petal dusts and transforming dry petal dust to liquid paint with a drop of vodka. Can be cleaned in the dishwasher.

Granular color (Sugarflair Colors Sugartex Granular Food Color)

Textured icing coloring to create lifelike pollen for stamen heads. My most frequently used Sugartex colors are "Pollen," "Mimosa," and "Black Magic."

Essential Household Tools

Being ready for a sugar flower project makes your work more efficient.

Digital gram scale

Use to measure accurate amounts of ingredients for both flower paste and baking.

Plastic wrap, resealable bags and containers

Always store flower paste tightly wrapped in plastic wrap and in an airtight container, especially after rolling it out or cutting petals. Air will dry out the paste in a short amount of time.

Paper towels

Use to absorb spilled or excess liquid egg white or moisture. Suitable to form a nest for drying sugar petals.

Butter knives

Used for dividing flower paste.

Bowls, various sizes

Use for measuring, dividing, or mixing ingredients.

Vodka or rejuvenator spirit (ethanol)

Adding a few drops of vodka to petal dust turns them into a liquid paint. If you don't want to use vodka, rejuvenator spirit is another option.

White parchment paper

A perfect surface for mixing petal dusts that doesn't absorb the dust like paper towels do, and paintbrushes slide over the surface with ease. It offers contrast to the petal dusts and provides a larger workspace than a painter's palette.

Cardboard fruit crates or foam flower drying tray

Foam trays specifically for sugar flower making have small cavities for cradling and drying petals. Cardboard fruit crates with curved cavities, such as ones that hold peaches, can be procured from grocers as a free resource. They are convenient for cradling and drying larger petals.

Flower Paste

This straightforward but precise recipe takes only a few minutes to assemble. This recipe makes enough to complete the five flower exercises in this book and, depending upon how thinly it is rolled, may allow you to create some extras. It can be scaled up to accommodate larger projects. The base is simply made with confectioners' sugar, liquid egg whites, and vegetable shortening combined with a gum powder to add strength. The result is a pliable and elastic paste that is easy to shape into simple or intricate botanical parts. For using as gum powder, there are various brands of food grade C.M.C. powder (carboxymethyl cellulose) or Tylose powder (a trade name of C.M.C. powder), which can be purchased online or at select craft stores. These will lend different textures and strengths, but I prefer and recommend PME C.M.C. / Tylo Petal Powder for this recipe, or Confectionery Arts International Tylose Powder as an alternative (see Resources, page 238).

The following proportions have been tested successfully in different parts of the world where climatic conditions and ingredient availability may influence the performance of the paste. Although it is not necessary for most locations, adding cream of tartar helps the finished flowers harden more reliably, especially in humid climates. In this recipe, I use only metric measurements for greater accuracy. A digital scale is essential for measuring the correct amount of each ingredient because even just a few grams' difference in the recipe can produce dramatically different (and undesirable) results! It's also vital to have a bowl scraper and plastic wrap within reach to prevent any unnecessary hardening because of prolonged air exposure. The power of a motor in a stand mixer is needed to prepare the paste, as opposed to using a hand mixer or kneading by hand. When preparing the paste and creating sugar flowers, avoid wearing clothing with fine fibers like cashmere or wool that may get into the paste and be impossible to remove as you work.

In a small bowl, whisk together the C.M.C. powder and cream of tartar and set aside.

In the bowl of a stand mixer fitted with the paddle attachment, sift in the confectioners' sugar, holding the sieve low in the bowl. Add the egg whites and begin mixing on low speed to just combine. Increase to medium speed and beat the mixture no longer than 3 minutes. During this time, you should observe it progress from a matte to a shiny and smooth appearance, like royal icing.

Scrape down the sides of the bowl and sprinkle in the C.M.C. powder and cream of tartar mixture. Beat on medium speed until incorporated, 30 to 40 seconds, until the mixture stiffens and regresses from a shiny to matte appearance.

Using a bowl scraper, transfer the flower paste to a clean work surface. Add the vegetable shortening and knead until it is fully incorporated, and the paste feels smooth and pliable, about 2 minutes. Time is of the essence at this point, as the C.M.C. powder quickly dries out the paste. Double-wrap the paste in plastic wrap or divide into smaller pieces and wrap separately.

Place the wrapped paste in a resealable plastic bag or lidded container and refrigerate at least overnight. Once refrigerated overnight, the wrapped flower paste can be removed from the refrigerator and stored at room temperature for 2 days, left in the refrigerator for up to 2 weeks, or frozen for up to 8 months in an airtight freezer bag.

Equipment

Whisk

Stand mixer with paddle attachment

Sieve

Bowl scraper

Plastic wrap

Resealable plastic bag or lidded container

Ingredients

17g C.M.C. or Tylose powder (see Resources, page 238)

¼ teaspoon cream of tartar (optional)

400g confectioners' sugar

70g liquid egg whites

14g vegetable shortening

Coloring Flower Paste and Creating the Flower Paste Balls

For most of the sugar flower projects, you will need to start with four flower paste balls: a "mother ball," an uncolored (white) ball, an ivory ball, and a lighter-colored version of the mother ball. Mixing bits of these four balls together allows you to create marbled flower petals with a realistic, natural appearance. The mother ball is the darkest-colored ball that you will create, and it acts as a base to be blended with other lighter-hued balls. As you work, the mother ball will lead the color gradient of petals for each sugar flower from darkest to lightest.

Each sugar flower project suggests specific amounts of paste for forming a suite of balls that can easily and quickly be measured using a digital gram scale. This suggested amount is meant as a guideline, and I hope that over time you will develop your own preferred quantities that reflect your flower model and process.

When removing paste from the refrigerator, bring it to room temperature for 1 hour before kneading, coloring, or modeling. When you begin making sugar flowers, you may need more paste to finish a flower than when you become more adept at rolling the petals thinly. If you find that you have not created enough paste to finish the flower, match the color of the mother ball to a new one to maintain consistency. Have the plastic wrap and container nearby to store the balls while you work and prevent the paste from drying out. Keep the container tightly sealed when not in use. The flower paste will keep wrapped and covered at room temperature for only two days before it hardens.

Equipment

Toothpick

Plastic wrap

Ingredients

Flower paste (page 190), in plastic wrap, room temperature

Various liquid gel colors (see Resources, page 238)

Various petal dusts (optional; see Resources, page 238)

To make one flower, unwrap the flower paste (reserving the plastic wrap) and pinch off the quantity specified in a flower recipe (see pages 198 to 227). Rewrap the remainder in plastic wrap and put aside for another flower.

To make a mother ball for a medium-to-large size flower with multiple petals, pinch off 2 tablespoons (50 g) of the unwrapped flower paste, form the remaining uncolored (white) paste into a ball, and wrap it in plastic wrap. Dip a toothpick into a jar of liquid gel color that is closest in hue to your fresh flower specimen or use two or three different liquid gel colors at a time to provide more depth. I always color the mother ball one shade lighter than the desired result so I can finish the flower with darker nuances of petal dust. Spread small amounts of gel onto the paste, keeping in mind the color will intensify as it rests.

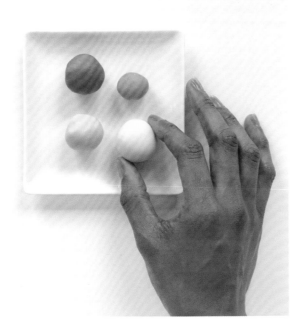

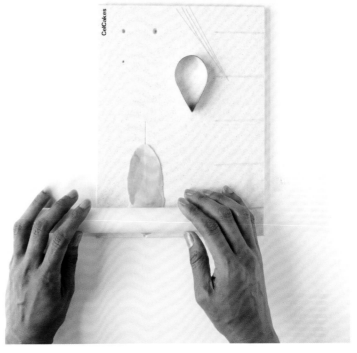

Knead the gel into the paste using your fingers, wrap the mother ball in plastic wrap, and set it aside in a covered container for 15 to 20 minutes for the paste to absorb the color. Adjust with more gel, if needed, or knead in more of the uncolored (white) paste to achieve a softer hue.

When you have achieved your desired color, roll the mother ball into a sphere, wrap it in plastic wrap, and replace it in the covered container.

To create an ivory ball to use for marbling, pinch off 1 tablespoon (25 g) of the uncolored (white) ball and mix with a small amount of ivory liquid gel color. Knead until completely mixed into the paste.

For most sugar flower projects, I recommend creating a lighter version of the mother ball for marbling. Pinch off half (1 tablespoon/25 g) of the mother ball and knead in some of the

uncolored (white) ball to soften the tone of the mother ball (see photo). You may also use some of the ivory ball to create a warmer look and tone down the color of the mother ball. Alternatively, powdered petal dust creates more subtle hues than liquid gel colors and can be kneaded into some additional uncolored (white) ball to create a lighter version of the mother ball. Whatever method you choose, this lighter ball will help you blend and achieve a marbled look for each petal.

Keep these four balls stored wrapped in plastic in the covered container at room temperature while you work, or up to 2 days.

Continued

PREPARING THE CENTERS OF FLOWERS

Depending upon the size of the center and the humidity of your environment, the centers of flowers consisting of the pistils and stamens need 24 to 48 hours to dry completely. Plan accordingly and don't skimp on this part of the process, or the center will slide off when proceeding with assembly. In my studio, I keep my sugar flowers on a piece of Styrofoam. I have completed flowers "blooming" and also flower centers dried and ready whenever I want to create petals and assemble a flower. To shorten the drying time, place sugar flower centers under a lamp with a warm bulb or pop them into a warm oven with the heat turned off.

For many flowers, it is okay to use premade store-bought stamens. You can make your own, but when you need a hundred, premade stamens are of excellent quality and might save your sanity!

MAKING THE PETALS

To create each petal of a flower, you will knead together small amounts of the mother ball with each of the other three balls to achieve a gradient of dark and bright petal colors to ones with more subtle tones. Depending upon the petal, you will want to use more or less of the uncolored (white), ivory, and subtler balls with the mother ball. If you want to make a darker petal, use more of the mother ball to marble with the other balls. If you want a lighter petal, mix a bit of the mother with more of the uncolored (white) ball for a lighter but cooler tone. Mix a bit of the ivory ball for a lighter but warmer tone, or use a combination of both white and ivory to create a bridge and blend with the mother ball. Refer to your fresh flower specimen often to mimic its color gradient, working your way from the color of the inside of the flower to the outer whorl of petals. Then proceed to the step-by-step instructions for creating a peony (page 198), garden rose (page 206), anemone (page 212), tulip (page 218), or cherry blossoms (page 224) for more specifics.

- When you are ready to roll out the paste, you may lightly dust a clean surface with cornstarch to prevent the paste from sticking if needed.

- Try not to massage the paste of each petal for too long or into one solid color—the perfect piece is slightly marbled before rolling it out onto the groove board and cutting into a petal shape.

- Mixing the mother ball with the other three balls ensures the flowers will have a natural color gradient that is lighter on the inside than the outside (or vice versa). Coloring petals this way gives you a head start when finishing petals in petal dust.

- Using a CelPin to thin petals takes some practice, but when mastered, it can achieve lifelike, cupped shapes that are so thin they become almost transparent. This doesn't have to apply to every flower; keeping petals thick can be more botanically correct for certain flowers.

- If you want to work more efficiently, it is possible to knead the leftover paste from the board and reuse it to roll new petals. Keep the cut petals stored in a resealable plastic bag, and if making many petals, work in batches of three to four. Freshly rolled petals are always easier to work with and less effort is needed to give them texture and definition.

- Create a few extra petals to experiment with applying dust and liquid colors to finish.

Continued

The Magic of the Little Black Ball

Create and store a little piece of flower paste colored in black in the refrigerator. Adding the tiniest drop of black paste to any other flower paste will give you a stunning vintage look (see pages 209 or 224).

USING PETAL DUST TO ADD NUANCE

When applying petal dust, it is important to use brushstrokes that begin from the base of the petal and extend toward the tip (if you want more color at the base of the petal) or from the tip of the petal to the middle (if you want more color on the tip of the petal). The golden rule is to always apply petal dust from the outside edges of the petal to the inside. Use a darker tone of petal dust than the petal when finishing the flower. It is this layered accumulation of color that will add lifelike interest to your flowers.

Use brown, gray, and dark green tones to add character and offer the illusion of wilt to a bloom. This aspect of coloring the petals and flowers is one of my favorite steps in the process of making sugar flowers, but I am hesitant to share with you my favorite colors. This journey is too much fun exploring yourself. Real flowers used as color reference are most delightful and recommended.

CREATING FOLIAGE FOR A COMPLETE LOOK

Leaves and sepals enhance the botanically correct appearance of sugar flowers and are essential to expressive arrangements and for decorating cakes. The basic technique is the same as making petals, but use silicone leaf veiners instead of petal veiners for more specialized textures (see instructions, page 210).

Starting with the pale green flower paste and coloring the leaves with dust is a perfect way to reflect the seasons: bright chartreuse green for spring; deep emerald green for summer; brown, red, and dark forest green tones for autumn. Dust a large begonia leaf in bold burgundy and green to speak with a striking presence in an arrangement. Embrace the creative opportunities of sugar foliage; the possibilities are endless for unique moments.

ASSEMBLING PETALS INTO COMPLETE FLOWERS

Taping petals together and turning them into a flower takes some time to master. I use the terms "half-width" and "whole-width" to describe Hamilworth floral tape.

Do not let the petals dry completely before taping them together to allow yourself some freedom to change the flower's appearance. Being able to fold or pinch a petal at the last minute can make an incredible difference in the resulting style. Although petals need to be secured tightly, try not to use too much tape in one place or around the base of the center to prevent bulkiness. I tape one petal at a time because I like to stay in control of the positioning. When adding multiple layers of wired petals, position them as close to the center and each other as you can to avoid what I call the "Christmas tree look," where the petals are secured with large gaps in between one another. To finish, use a brush with a touch of brown, red, or dark green petal dust to soften or accentuate a stem that has been taped.

PRESERVING SUGAR FLOWERS

Storing your sugar flower creations is simple, with a few considerations. If exposed to direct sunlight, the colors may fade; but without extreme humidity they will last for years to come. When stored under a glass dome, however, they provide permanent and exquisite decor. Because I play with my flowers so often, I have created a "sugar garden" where I keep them uncovered and mounted on large pieces of sturdy foam. As I create and welcome each new sugar flower, my heart grows full of satisfaction all over again.

Sugar Flower Peony

When peonies are in bloom, nature offers a six-week window of indulgence from the middle of spring to the beginning of summer. Re-creating peonies in sugar extends this short season of pleasure and provides the option of revisiting their beauty whenever we like. Composed of paper-thin petals in sumptuous colors, peonies add an air of elegance to any room or a gesture of opulence to a celebration cake. I have yet to meet a person who doesn't like peonies, and whenever florals are chosen for weddings or celebrations, it is always a favorite—I consider peonies the "Queen of Flowers" for a reason. For many, fresh peonies are expensive to purchase at the market, but creating them in sugar is an investment that provides years of enjoyment.

Herbaceous and tree peonies come in a vast array of colors and flower forms ranging from just a few petals to dozens. The following is an example of how to create a single flower of 'Coral Charm', a favorite peony among many. To mimic this flower's sumptuous quality, around forty petals are necessary for assembly. This may seem daunting at first, but the repetition is an opportunity to become increasingly comfortable with the process and hone your skills—each new petal will be a satisfying improvement over the last. If, however, you prefer a shorter commitment, the bowl-shaped satin white petals of 'Jan Van Leeuwen' may offer a simpler alternative. If you prefer the ruffled yellow 'Bartzella' peony instead, the biggest difference will be in the petal dusts necessary for making its cheery petals. Choose a peony that inspires you and try to remain open to the lessons learned along the way. Creating sugar flowers gets easier with time, and the discoveries you make will only encourage a greater appreciation of nature's wonders.

As with all sugar flowers, make and completely dry the flower center in advance before creating and assembling the petals. When creating a bouquet of sugar peonies, varying the number of pistils for each flower will have a more natural effect in the overall presentation. Regardless of how many petals you create, keep them stored in a resealable plastic bag while you work to prevent a skin from forming on the surface.

The Essential Sugar Flower Tool Kit (page 184)

Essential Household Tools (page 188)

½ cup (170g) flower paste

Liquid gel colors (yellow, orange, pink, pale green)

PME cutting wheel

Ball tools, fine and medium to large

Scratch wire brush

Petal dusts (yellow, orange, pale pink, peony pink, and cyclamen, dark brown, green, forest green, and burgundy)

Premade peony stamens

Craft glue

Sugertex Granular Food Color ("Pollen" and "Mimosa")

Peony petal cutters, small, medium, and large (2-inch, 2¼-inch, and 2¾-inch)

Peony leaf cutter, medium (3-inch)

Peony silicone petal veiners, medium and large (2½-inch and 3-inch)

Peony silicone leaf veiner, large (3½-inch)

Continued

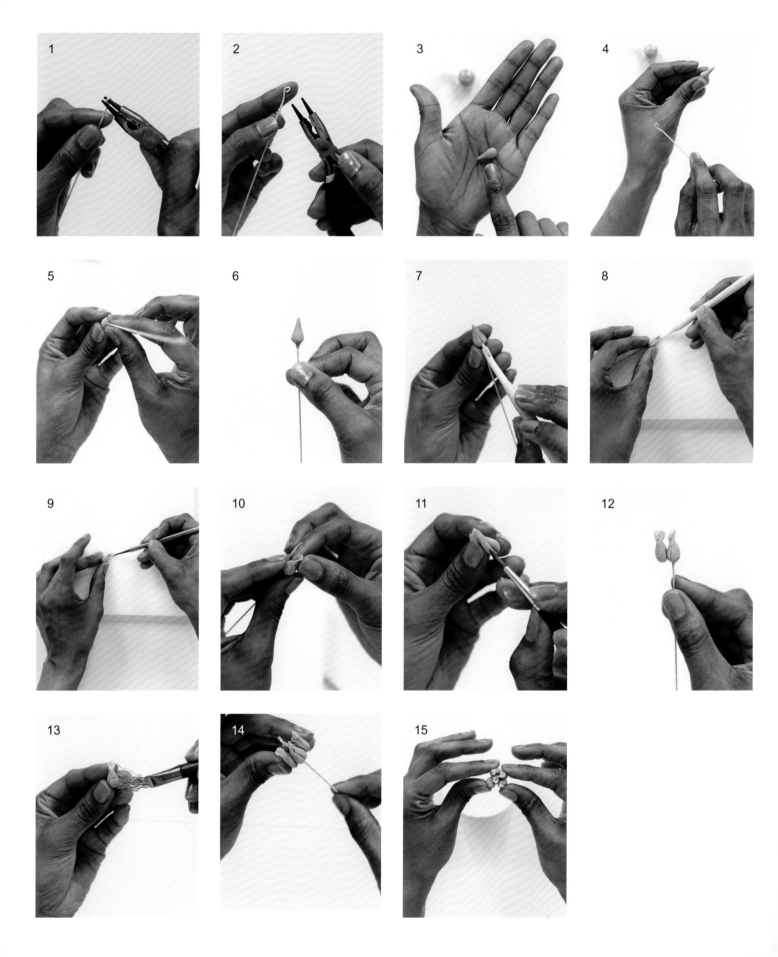

MAKE THE FLOWER PASTE BALLS

Using ⅓ cup plus 2 tablespoons (140 g) of the flower paste, make the four flower paste balls according to page 192. Use a blend of yellow, orange, and pink liquid gel colors to achieve a coral color for the mother ball. In addition to these, use ⅛ cup (30g) of the uncolored (white) ball to create a ball using pale green liquid gel color using the same method.

CREATE THE PISTILS

To make the first pistil, cut an 18-gauge floral wire in half using wire cutters. Grip the top of the wire with needle-nose pliers, and using some force, turn the pliers to form a small oblong closed hook about ¼-inch long. Set aside. *(1, 2)*

Massage a small piece (about 1 teaspoon/10g) of light green flower paste until it is malleable, adding a touch of vegetable shortening if the paste feels dry. Roll a pea-size ball in the palm of your hand. With your index finger, add some pressure to one side of the ball and roll it into a cone shape. *(3)* Dip the hook of the wire in egg white and wipe away any excess. *(4)*

Dust your fingertips with cornstarch to absorb any excess egg white. Insert the hook into the pistil and push it toward the pointed end of the cone. *(5, 6)* Pinch the belly of the cone to secure it to the wire. With the small end of a cutting wheel, make an indentation in the pistil to add texture. *(7)*

Place the pistil on a flower foam pad. Hold the base of the cone in place, and with the wide-end of a Dresden tool, flatten and elongate the top of the pistil to form a concave shape. *(8)* Dip the small end of a ball tool in cornstarch and stroke from the tip of the pistil out and over the pad to create a thin and frilly edge. *(9)* Holding the pistil's belly, twist the top of the pistil a quarter turn. *(10)*

Repeat steps 3 to 10 to make an additional pistil. Using a small paintbrush, dab a small amount of egg white on one side of the pistil and gently press it into the central pistil mounted on the wire. *(11, 12)* Use a paper towel to carefully remove any excess egg white that would resist absorbing petal dust.

Repeat steps 3 to 10 once more. Use a scratch wire brush against the sides of the new pistil to give it some texture. *(13)* Dab egg white on one side of the new pistil and secure it to the center pistil mounted on the wire. *(14)* Always attach each newly formed pistil to the center before creating the next pistil.

Mount the wire into a Styrofoam block and gently push all the pistils together to secure the center. *(15)* For maximum support, keep the hook of the wire neatly in place in the center pistil. Dry the pistils completely, 24 to 48 hours, before proceeding to step 16.

Continued

BUNDLE THE STAMENS AND ASSEMBLE THE CENTER

Gather approximately 100 premade peony stamens and arrange them into bundles of 10. Dollop craft glue onto a piece of paper and dip the middle of one bundle into the glue. *(16)* Combine with another bundle of stamens, pressing the middles together with your thumb and index finger. Repeat until all the bundles are glued together. While sticky, use scissors to cut the middle and create two groups. *(17)* Press the glued sides together.

Using a palette tray, mix various shades of yellow and orange petal dust together to create a natural pollen color. Using a dry brush, dust the stamen stems and anthers (on the tips of the stamens) with the mixture. *(18)* Pour some "Pollen" and "Mimosa" granular color into the tray, and using the back of a spoon, crush the crystals to create a fine texture. Stir in some of the yellow-orange petal dust mixture to create your flower pollen. Dab small amounts of egg white onto the anthers and dip them into the flower pollen. *(19)* Using a clean dry brush, apply green petal dust onto the dried pistils, stroking from the bottom toward the tip. *(20)*

Using a dry brush, apply a pale pink petal dust to the top of the pistils. To make a liquid paint, add a drop of vodka to a well of the palette tray and stir in some cyclamen or peony pink petal dust. Using a small paintbrush, apply the paint to the top of each pistil in short and even accent strokes. *(21)* While the stamens are still sticky, slide the wire of the pistils through the center of the stamens until the bottom of the pistils rest neatly against the middle. *(22)*

Use a piece of whole-width floral tape to secure the stamens and pistils together in a bundle. Press and hold the beginning of the tape to the center of the bundle with your thumb and index finger. While simultaneously twisting the wire, stretch the tape as you spin and wrap it around the wire. After stretching it a few times around the center bundle, stretch and hold the tape diagonally while spinning and wrapping it all the way down the wire. *(23, 24)* Using the back of a paintbrush, curl the stamens around the center. *(25)*

CUT THE FLOWER PETALS

Knead a grape-size piece of soft coral pink flower paste until malleable. Secure the paste to the bottom of a groove board by pressing it over a groove. Using a rolling pin, extend the paste lengthwise over the groove until it is smooth and even. *(26)* At this point, the paste should be about twice as thick as the desired result. Gauging this takes some practice, but after finishing a few petals, you will have a better sense of the process. Peel the paste away from the groove board and position it upside up on a flat surface of the board. Using a small peony petal cutter, cut a petal with the vein positioned in the middle. *(27)* Rub your thumb over the edges of the cutter to clean the edge and release the petal from the cutter. *(28)*

Place the petal immediately in a resealable plastic bag and repeat two or three more times. It is possible to massage the leftover paste and quickly reuse it to roll new petals. When working your way through the flower's petals, you may wish to combine the mother ball with more or less of the other balls to create a lighter or darker colored petal. Remember that you will also have petal dust to help achieve subtle nuance in the petals.

SHAPE THE PETALS

Cut a 28-gauge wire into four equal-size pieces for smaller and medium petals, or three equal-size pieces for larger petals. You will need one piece of wire for each petal. Retrieve one petal from the plastic bag, and tightly reseal the bag. Dip a wire in egg white and wipe away any excess. Carefully insert the wire into the tapered end of the petal through the length of the vein. *(29)* Place the vein-side facing up onto a flower foam pad. Using some pressure, slide a CelPin over the entire length of the petal—do not stop short before the edge of the petal, but let the tool glide over and onto the pad instead. Avoid flattening the vein in the middle so the wire will stay securely in place. *(30)* Once the petal has increased in size, firmly slide the CelPin in a continuous motion over the edges of the petal to

Continued

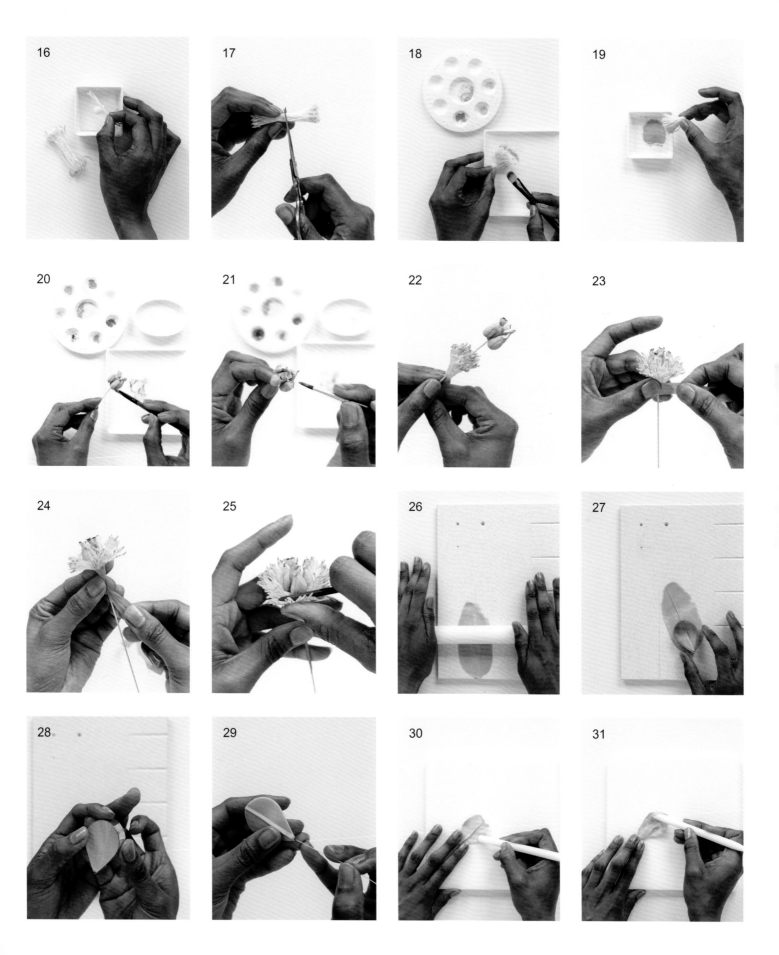

create a cupped and frilly appearance. *(31)* Flip the petal over and thin it out on the front-facing side until it is almost translucent.

Transfer the petal to a peony veiner and close the top. *(32)* Set the veiner on a hard surface and give it a firm push with both hands. Remove the petal from the veiner and cradle it to encourage a cupped shape. *(33)* Transfer the petal to the groove board. Using the wide end of a Dresden tool, thin the edges to encourage them to curl inward. *(34)* In a few of the petals, snip V-shaped pieces from the top edge before finishing their thinning. *(35)* This will enhance the petal with an irregular-shaped edge for more natural movement. Fold and press a crease at the bottom of each petal to force a cupped shape. *(36)* Repeat along the sides, close to the top of the petal, to create more irregularity. As you finish each petal, set it aside in a cardboard fruit crate or foam flower drying tray to dry.

Repeat steps 26 to 36 to make the next three or four petals. To create this peony example, I suggest making a total of about thirteen small inner petals, nine medium petals, and twelve large petals for the outside whorl, using the appropriate size cutters for each set of petals. This amount makes a very full, impressive flower and allows plenty of practice.

MAKE THE SEPALS

Roll a grape-size ball of light green sugar paste in the palm of your hand until smooth with no creases remaining. Insert a 28-gauge wire into the ball so it extends about ½ to ¾ inch through to the other side. Using a CelPin, roll the ball flat over the smooth surface of a groove board. *(37)* Transfer it to a flower foam pad, and using the CelPin, thin out the edges with the same process as for the petals. Place the sepal into the peony petal silicone veiner. Position the top of the veiner and press firmly.

Transfer the sepal to your hand and pinch the top between your thumb and index finger to encourage a cupped shape. *(38)* Set aside and repeat once more.

Dry the petals and sepals for 30 to 60 minutes, depending upon the humidity of the room, before adding petal dust and assembling. The petals should be dry enough to absorb the dust but still moist and pliable for assembly.

Using a dry brush, first apply various tones of yellow petal dust to the inside base of the petals. Next, apply various tones of pale pink, peony pink, and cyclamen petal dusts at the bottom of the petal, finishing with light touches of yellow and orange. When applying petal dust, always brush from either end of the petal toward the middle to achieve a natural graduation of color.

MAKE THE LEAVES

To create the foliage, see "Create the Leaves" (page 210), using a peony leaf cutter and veiner instead. Only one or two leaves are necessary.

ASSEMBLE THE FLOWER

Assemble the flower graduating from the smallest petals of the inner whorl to the largest. Using the floral tape on the flower's center as a guideline, secure the wire of the first inner petal using a small piece of half-width floral tape. *(39, 40)* Try not to use excessive amounts of floral tape to prevent bulkiness and tape them as close to the center and each other as possible. Finish the flower by taping the sepals and a peony leaf or two below the last layer of petals. *(41)*

Using a brush, add petal dust to the back of the petals, stroking from the base to the edges. Be bold when coloring the base of the peony. Touches of dark brown, forest green, and burgundy will make the peony flower look natural.

Sugar Flower Garden Rose

No flower represents love and romance like a garden-grown rose. Each summer, I eagerly wait for them to emerge on my rooftop and anticipate each compelling stage of their evolving display. Some wild roses have only five petals and convey sweet simplicity. Others with multiple petals take more time to create but can easily add romance and drama when used in a fresh flower arrangement. My favorite is when the petals have become blousy and their center is revealed, so vulnerable and passionate. Experiment using different size and shape rose cutters (even heart-shaped ones) and use various petal dusts. The centers are typically yellow to green, and the stamens range from yellow to orange with tinges of red.

A rose created in sugar is incredibly versatile, and I always have them on my table. They are one of the most difficult flowers for others to distinguish from the real thing, and I love to keep people guessing! Creating a rose with individually taped petals allows you to manipulate the flower to suit your needs in an arrangement or as a single flower on a cake. Close the petals for a bud filled with promise, or spread the petals open to catch the light. The garden rose is a sugar flower I never consider finished because you can always reshape, pinch, and play with the petals to create a new look.

As with all sugar flowers, make and completely dry the flower center in advance before creating and assembling the petals. It is possible to purchase premade stamens, but making your own for this flower out of thread is relatively simple and provides a much more natural look. Although coarse sandpaper will work, a clean pedi foot file reserved for sugar flower making is unmatched for fluffing the stamens and providing extra surface for receiving pollen. Tweak the pollen with different tones of yellow or even red petal dust for a natural look. To assist in drying the petals, make a nest made from paper towels by folding each piece into a triangle. Loosely roll up the triangle as you would a bandanna, beginning at the widest side, and finishing toward the pointed end. Form a circle and tie the ends together. Store the nests in a box to reuse as necessary.

The Essential Sugar Flower Tool Kit (page 184)

Essential Household Tools (page 188)

¼ cup (80g) flower paste

Liquid gel colors (lemon yellow, claret, dusty rose, ivory, and green)

Petal dusts (dusky pink, pink candy, rose, lavender drop, champagne, brown, tangerine, primrose, yellow, autumn gold, mustard, vine, and leaf green)

Heavy-duty thread

Sugartex Granular Food Color ("Pollen")

Rose petal cutter, small, medium, and large (1¼-inch, 2-inch, and 2¼-inch)

Rose leaf cutter, medium (2-inch)

Rose silicone petal veiner, extra extra large (2½-inch)

Rose silicone leaf veiner, medium (2½-inch)

Pedi foot file or coarse sandpaper

Continued

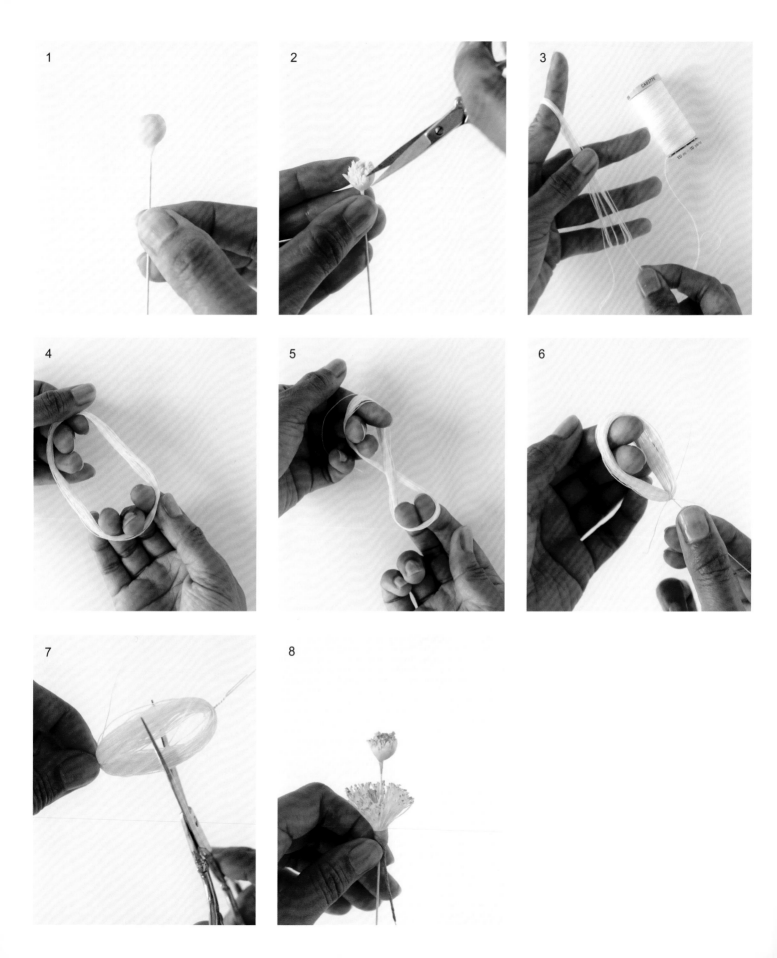

1

2

3

4

5

6

7

8

MAKE THE FLOWER PASTE BALLS

Using 2 tablespoons/50 g of flower paste, create the four flower paste balls according to the instructions on page 192. Use a blend of lemon yellow, claret, and dusky rose liquid gel colors to create a coral-colored mother ball, with a pinch of the magic black ball (page 196) for a vintage look. In addition to these, make one small (1 teaspoon/10g) ball with lemon yellow liquid gel color, and one small (2 teaspoons/20g) ball with green.

CREATE THE CENTER

Cut a 20-gauge floral wire in half, and using needle-nose pliers, create a closed hook (see peony instructions page 201, steps 1 and 2). Knead a small piece (about 1 teaspoon/10g) of ivory and lemon-yellow flower paste until it is malleable, adding a touch of shortening if the paste feels dry. Roll a pea-size ball in the palm of your hand. With your index finger, add some pressure to one side of the ball and roll the pistil into a cone shape. Dip the hook of the wire in egg white and wipe away any excess. Insert the hook into the belly of the pistil and push it toward the top. Ensure the hook is firmly in place and squeeze close the base of the pistil around the wire. Dip your fingertips into the cornstarch and hold the base of the flower center (ovary) while twisting the wire to taper and remove any excess paste. *(1)* Using ultra-fine embroidery scissors, add texture to the pistil by snipping the paste with tiny cuts. *(2)* Insert the wire into the Styrofoam block and set it aside to dry completely, 12 to 24 hours.

CREATE THE STAMENS

Cut a 28-gauge wire in two and set aside. Wind the thread approximately sixty times around four slightly spread fingers to create a bundled loop. *(3, 4)* Twist the circle to create a figure eight and fold it in half to create a smaller circle. *(5)* Twist a piece of wire tightly around one side of the circle and repeat on the opposite side. *(6)* Cut the circle in half, leaving you with two bunches of stamens. *(7)* Use a piece of whole-width floral tape to tie each bunch together around its base to form a single bundle. To fluff the thread, rub the top of the bundle over a pedi foot file or coarse sandpaper a few times. Using a dry brush, apply yellow to autumn gold petal dusts to the stamens. Pour the "Pollen" granular color into a small bowl for your flower pollen. Brush the tops of the stamens with a small amount of egg white and dip them into the flower pollen. Set aside to dry for about 5 minutes.

ASSEMBLE THE CENTER

With a dry brush, apply a combination of leaf green, vine, brown, and yellow petal dusts from the ovary toward the top of the pistil. Lightly brush the top with egg white and dip it in the pollen. Set it aside to dry for a few minutes.

Poke and slide the wire of the flower center through the bundle of stamens until the center rests neatly in the middle. *(8)* Use a small piece of whole-width floral tape to secure the wires to the stem and set aside.

Continued

CREATE THE PETALS

Begin by creating the smallest petal: knead a grape-size piece of marbled pink flower paste until it is malleable. Secure the paste to the bottom of a groove board by pressing it over a groove. Use a rolling pin to extend the paste over the groove until it is smooth and even. *(9)* Peel the paste away from the groove board and position it vein side up on a flat surface of the board. Using a rose cutter, cut out a petal with the vein positioned in the middle. *(10)* Place the petal immediately in a resealable plastic bag and repeat two or three more times. Cut two to three (28-gauge) wires into four equal-size pieces each. Depending on the rose, you will need thirteen to fifteen pieces total, one for each petal. Retrieve one petal from the plastic bag and tightly reseal the bag. Dip a piece of wire in egg white and wipe away any excess. Insert the wire into the tapered end of the petal through the length of the vein.

Place the petal with the vein side up onto the flat surface of your groove board. Slide a CelPin over the petal with considerable pressure to thin and increase the petal's size. *(11)* Repeat to create a graduation of small, medium, and larger size rose petals, three or four at a time, keeping them sealed in a plastic bag until you are ready to shape. For this rose I cut out one very small petal, nine medium-size petals, and five large rose petals.

SHAPE THE PETALS

Working in batches of three or four, place the first petal with the vein side facing up onto your flower foam pad. Using your CelPin, continue thinning out the petals to significantly increase them in size, embracing any tears or holes that appear organic and interesting. *(12)* Transfer the petal to the veiner and close the top. Set the veiner on a hard surface and give it a firm push with both hands. *(13)* Remove the petal from the veiner. Transfer the petal to the groove board, and using the wide end of a Dresden tool, thin the top edges of the petal to encourage them to curl outward. To achieve a cupped shape, fold a crease at the base of the petal (see peony instructions, page 205, step 36). Gently place each shaped petal in a paper towel nest (see page 206) and set aside to dry for about 30 minutes, or until slightly dry but still malleable. *(14)*

COLOR THE PETALS

Using a dry brush, apply various tones of yellow petal dust to the inside base of the petals. *(15)* Apply various tones of pink, red, and even brown at the top of the petal. Always brush from either end of the petal toward the inside to achieve a natural graduation of color.

ASSEMBLE THE FLOWER

Attach the smallest petal to the flower center with a small piece of whole-width floral tape. *(16)* Continue attaching petals in increasing size, manipulating them gently to fold into and embrace each other, ending with the largest petals for the outside whorl. *(17, 18)* To prevent a bulky stem, avoid taping all the way down the wire with each petal. To finish, use a dry brush to apply red petal dusts to the back base of the rose and adjust the petals as needed.

CREATE THE LEAVES (OPTIONAL)

Cut a 28-gauge wire in half. Using a rolling pin, roll out a marbled piece of green flower paste on your groove board. *(19)* Using a rose leaf cutter, cut out a leaf. *(20)* Insert a wire into the round end of the leaf the full length of the vein. Using a CelPin, thin the leaf on your flower foam pad and transfer it to a leaf veiner and close the top. Set the veiner on a hard surface and give it a firm push with both hands. *(21)*

Carefully lift the leaf from the veiner and transfer to a flower foam pad. Using a ball tool, soften the edges for a natural look. *(22)* Place the leaf on a fruit crate or foam flower drying tray, and set aside to dry for about 30 minutes, or until slightly dry but still malleable. Repeat as desired. Add the leaves, with the pointed end facing upward, to the base of the flower with tape and apply dark green to brown petal dusts to finish. *(23)*

Sugar Flower Anemone

A flower that closes its petals at nightfall to protect it from harm creates a special kind of poetry in an arrangement. Also known as the windflower, the anemone is said to cling to life for a brief and tense moment before it is lost to time. If an anemone were a character in a play, it would command attention with the bravery and confidence that living a short and fast life surely cultivates. Thankfully, creating these flowers in sugar allows us to cling to their beauty a bit longer.

Despite the variety, I often sculpt anemones with dramatic black centers, and they are one of my favorites to arrange with fresh flowers. To mimic the unique texture of the centers, begin with premade white hammerhead stamens, adding a mixture of aubergine (dark purple) and dark brown petal dusts to the pollen to create nuance and depth.

As with all sugar flowers, make and completely dry the flower center before creating and assembling the petals. When making more than one anemone, vary the size of the central mound and the number of petals to avoid uniformity and achieve a more natural appearance. Although I prefer using an anemone veiner to create the petals, a rose veiner can be used instead.

The Essential Sugar Flower Tool Kit (page 184)

Essential Household Tools (page 188)

2 tablespoons plus 1 teaspoon (50g) flower paste

Scratch wire brush

Angled tweezers

Craft knife

Sugartex Granular Food Color ("Black Magic")

Craft glue

Premade white hammerhead stamens

Petal dusts (black, aubergine/dark purple, brown, champagne, shadow gray, dusky pink, rose, skin tone, plum, grape violet, deep purple, African violet, and leaf green)

Anemone or rose petal cutter, small (1½-inch)

Anemone silicone petal veiner, medium (2-inch)

MAKE THE FLOWER PASTE BALLS

Use the flower paste to prepare only two balls for this project according to the instructions on page 192: a two-teaspoon (20g) uncolored (white) ball and a two-teaspoon (20g) mother ball using a combination of soft pink petal dusts rather than liquid gel colors to achieve only a hint of color. You don't need to create an ivory ball or a lighter-colored version of the mother ball for this flower. In addition to these, create another smaller (1 teaspoon/10g) ball using a combination of black, brown, and deep purple liquid gel colors.

CREATE THE CENTRAL MOUND

Cut a 20-gauge floral wire in half and, using needle-nose pliers, create a closed hook (see peony instructions, page 201, steps 1 and 2). Knead the dark-colored flower paste until it is malleable, adding a touch of shortening if the paste feels dry. Roll the paste into a smooth ball in the palm of your hand.

Continued

1

2

3

4

5

6

7

8

Dip the hook of the wire into egg white and wipe away any excess. Insert the hook into the center of the ball almost to the top. Ensure the hook is firmly in place and squeeze close the base of the ball around the wire. Dip your fingertips into the cornstarch and pinch the bottom of the ball while twisting the wire to remove any excess paste and taper the ball. *(1)* Flatten the top of the ball with your fingers.

Using the scratch wire brush, create texture on the ball. Using the angled tweezers, make grooves on the top and around the sides of the ball. *(2)* With the craft knife, slice indentations from the center to the outside rim of the ball. *(3)* Insert the wire into the Styrofoam block and set it aside to dry completely, 12 to 24 hours, before applying the pollen.

Pour the "Black Magic" granular color into a small bowl for your flower pollen. Lightly brush the top of the flower center with egg white and dip it into the flower pollen. *(4)* Dry before moving on to step five, 10 to 20 minutes.

ASSEMBLE THE CENTER

Glue one bunch of white hammerhead stamens together according to the peony instructions on page 202, step 16. Using scissors, cut the sticky stamens in half to create two bundles. *(5)* Set one aside for using to make an additional anemone. Dip a paintbrush in vodka and use it to apply aubergine (dark purple) and black petal dusts to the anthers. *(6)* Dry for a few minutes before very lightly brushing with egg white. Dip the anthers in the black pollen. *(7)*

While the stamens are still slightly sticky, slide the wire of the central mound through the center of the stamens, until the base rests neatly among them. *(8)* Use a piece of half-width floral tape to secure the stamens and center together in a bundle. Curl the stamens inward with the back of a thin brush.

Continued

CREATE THE PETALS (TEPALS)

Cut two or three 28-gauge wires into four equal-size pieces each. Depending on the anemone, you will need eight to ten pieces total, one for each petal. Secure a small piece of pale pink flower paste to the bottom of a groove board by pressing it over a groove. Using a rolling pin, extend the paste lengthwise over the groove until it is smooth and even. *(9)* Peel the paste away from the board and position it with the vein facing up on a flat surface of the board. For a more delicate finish, press your CelPin at right angles to flatten the groove at what will be the top of your petal. *(10)* Use an anemone cutter to cut out a petal with the vein positioned in the middle. Dip a wire in egg white and wipe off any excess. Insert the wire through the length of the vein. *(11)*

Using your CelPin, thin the petal, vein side up, on a flower foam pad until it appears somewhat translucent. *(12)* Transfer the petal to the veiner and close the top. Set the veiner on a hard surface and give it a firm push with both hands. *(13)* Remove the petal from the veiner. To encourage the petal to curl naturally, slide a Dresden tool along one side of the top of the petal. *(14)* (Repeat this with only a few additional petals.) Transfer the petal to a cardboard fruit crate or foam flower drying tray to dry and repeat steps 9 to 15 for the additional petals. *(15)* For a more organic appearance, create a few curled petals as if they are unfolding from the center. Set the drying tray full of petals aside until they are stiff but still somewhat malleable, 30 to 45 minutes.

COLOR THE PETALS

Using a dry brush, apply a mix of pink and purple petal dusts to the petals in a graduated scale, brushing from the base of the petal outward toward the tip. *(16)*

ASSEMBLE THE FLOWER

Beginning with the smallest petals, tape the first petal to the flower center. *(17)* Add three to four more petals to the first whorl, taping one at a time to maintain control over their placement. Evenly space and secure the last petals. *(18)* To finish, apply bold strokes of petal dusts to the back base of the flower with a dry brush. *(19)*

Sugar Flower Tulip

The image of this celebrated flower has been ingrained into our culture since it landed on our shores, most notably by the Dutch Masters in their paintings. The tulip's rise in importance mirrored the obsession to control nature and flaunt possession of its rarest irregularities. It has helped shape our economy and influenced fashionable trends in pottery and entertaining. The joyful, whimsical character of tulips has transfixed admirers for centuries and remains a favorite addition to any contemporary fresh flower arrangement or celebration cake.

Tulips are one of the first flowers to bloom in the spring, and I love welcoming them into our home when they arrive in the markets or bloom on my terrace. No other flower encourages my creativity like the tulip, as they add a graceful touch to any arrangement. Re-creating them in sugar is to study movement, and the flames of their petals indulge my love of painting. There are so many varieties that really push using color, an activity that I can never resist. There is no gradient with the six petals of the frilly 'Parrot Peach' tulip that is referenced here, but marbling the flower paste is still important because each petal is so irregular and unlike the others. As with most sugar flowers, make and completely dry the flower center in advance before creating and assembling the petals.

The Essential Sugar Flower Tool Kit (page 184)

Essential Household Tools (page 188)

2 tablespoons plus 2½ teaspoons (60g) flower paste

Liquid gel colors (peach, pink, lemon yellow, ivory, and light green)

Petal dusts (primrose, lemon yellow, autumn gold, salmon, apricot, dusty rose, tangerine, skin tone, poppy red, cream, vine, leaf green, forest green, chocolate, brown, and aubergine/dark purple)

Angled tweezers

Sugartex Granular Food Color ("Black Magic")

Tulip petal cutter, large (2½-inch)

Parrot tulip silicone petal veiner, large (3-inch)

Ultra-fine ball tool

Scriber needle or bamboo skewer

6 large spoons

MAKE THE FLOWER PASTE BALLS

Using 2 tablespoons plus 1 teaspoon/50 g of flower paste, create the four flower paste balls according to instructions on page 192. Use a combination of peach, pink, and lemon-yellow liquid gel colors to achieve an apricot color for the mother ball. In addition to these flower balls, use light green gel colors to marble 1 teaspoon (10g) ball of paste.

MAKE THE PISTIL

Cut a 20-gauge floral wire in half, and using needle-nose pliers, create a closed hook (see peony instructions, page 201, steps 1 and 2). Knead the light green flower paste until it is malleable, adding a touch of shortening if the paste feels dry. Roll a pinch of this paste into an oblong pistil in the palm of your hand. Apply pressure in the middle with your index and middle finger and elongate it to about 1¼ inches. Dip the hook of your wire in egg white and wipe off any excess. Insert the hook into the base of the pistil and push it to the top. Ensure the hook

Continued

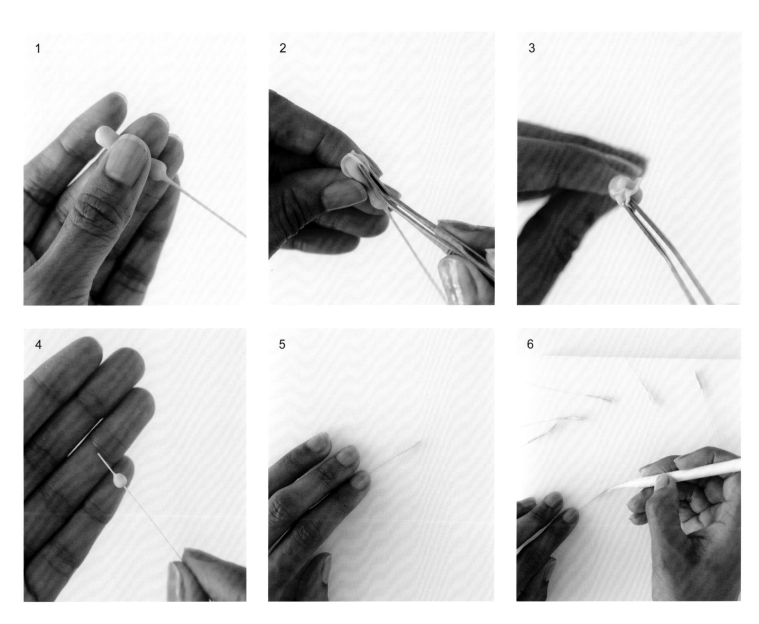

is firmly in place and squeeze close the base of the pistil (ovary) around the wire. Dip your fingertips into the cornstarch and grip the ovary while twisting the wire to taper and remove any excess paste. The pistil should be slim in the middle and thicker at the top and bottom. *(1)*

Gently flatten the top of the pistil. Using the tweezers, define the stigma: pinch three ridges beginning at the top of the pistil that taper down the sides and smooth out in the middle. *(2)* Pinch each ridge at the top to create a slight twist. *(3)* Insert the wire into the Styrofoam block and set it aside to dry completely, 12 to 24 hours, before moving on to step four.

CREATE SIX STAMENS WITH ANTHERS

Cut two 28-gauge wires into five even pieces. Knead a small ball of ivory paste and pinch off a piece that is the size of a small pearl on a pushpin. Roll it into a ball and insert a piece of the wire through the ball, extending 1 inch from the top. *(4)* Roll the ball on its side to elongate the tip into an anther. *(5)* Place the stamen on a flower foam pad, and using the thin end of a Dresden tool, create a groove from the middle to the end lengthwise. *(6)* Create five additional stamens and leave to dry completely, about an hour.

Using a dry paintbrush, apply petal dusts to the pistil. Use darker green or brown dusts on the ovary and brighter green or yellow dusts closer to the stigma. With a fine paintbrush, apply a small amount of egg white to the ridges of the stigma. Pour the "Black Magic" granular color into a small bowl for your flower pollen and swirl the stigma through the flower pollen. Set aside to dry for a few minutes. With a dry paintbrush, apply some aubergine (dark purple) petal dust to the stamens. Using a fine paintbrush, apply a small amount of egg white onto the anthers, avoiding the groove. Pour some more "Black Magic" granular color into a small bowl and swirl the anthers through this flower pollen. Set the stamens aside to dry for a few minutes.

ASSEMBLE THE STAMENS AND PISTIL

Use a short piece of half-width floral tape to secure the wire of the first stamen to the base of the pistil, stretching the tape to release the glue. *(7)* Repeat with the remaining stamens. Finish with a longer piece of tape stretching three-quarters down the wire and set aside.

Continued

MAKE THE PETALS (TEPALS)

Cut two 28-gauge wires into four equal-size pieces each. Depending on the tulip, you will need a minimum of six pieces, one for each petal. Using the flower paste balls, create a grape-size piece of marbled ivory-apricot paste, kneading until it is malleable. Secure the paste to the bottom of a groove board by pressing it over a groove. Use a rolling pin to extend the paste lengthwise over the groove until it is smooth and even. *(8)* Peel the paste away from the groove board and position it vein side up on a flat surface of the board.

Using a tulip cutter, cut out a petal with the vein positioned in the middle. Dip a wire in egg white and wipe off any excess. Insert the wire into the tapered end of the vein and push it three-quarters through the length of the vein. *(9)* Place the petal vein side facing upward onto a flower foam pad. Slide a CelPin over the petal with pressure to thin and increase the size of the petal. *(10)*

SHAPE THE PETALS

Transfer the petal to the veiner and close the top. Set the veiner on a hard surface and give it a firm push with both hands. *(11)* Remove the petal from the veiner. Transfer the petal to the groove board. Using the wide end of a Dresden tool, thin the edges of the petal to encourage a cloven appearance. *(12, 13)*

Place the petal on the flower foam pad. Using an ultra-fine ball tool, apply gentle pressure to occasionally frill the petal, embracing any tears as a natural representation of the parrot tulip. *(14)* Use a scriber needle tool to gently curl petals inward or outward. *(15)* Nestle the petal into a spoon and set aside to dry until you are ready to dust and assemble. Repeat steps 8 to 16 to create five additional petals. Set the spoons aside until the petals are stiff but still somewhat malleable, 40 to 60 minutes. *(16)*

COLOR THE PETALS

Using a dry brush, apply a mix of petal dusts to the petals. *(17)* To mimic the flames of a parrot tulip, use a touch of vodka with the petal dusts to create a liquid paint. Using a fine brush, apply strokes of liquid color to the tips of the petals. If necessary, apply a light application of petal dust over the flames to soften.

ASSEMBLE THE TULIP

Secure the wire of the first petal to the base of the center with whole-width floral tape. *(18)* Follow with two more evenly spaced petals, taped one at a time. *(19)* Secure the remaining three petals in between the first layer. *(20)* To finish, apply a mix of petal dusts to the back base of the tulip.

Sugar Flower Cherry Blossoms

If there is one word to describe a cherry blossom, it would be "enchanting." A whole tree in bloom can be breathtaking, but even one branch can inspire magic. I try and evoke this sense of awe in everyday life and always have stems of sugar cherry blossoms nearby to help me along. Even with only a few, these small accent flowers make any arrangement playful. Their delicate blooms not only fill in the gaps, but they also amplify the presence of large focal flowers and light up the composition with a sense of wonder.

Once the flowers are formed, each is taped onto a central stem in a trailing, natural way. Using this shaping and taping technique will open the door to vast possibilities, including small blue accent flowers for the arrangement on page 175. Follow the same method as outlined here but try using a petunia cutter to create florets of lilacs or hydrangeas instead. Depending on the flower, you can sometimes omit creating the stamens and simply form a hook.

The Essential Sugar Flower Tool Kit (page 184)

Essential Household Tools (page 188)

⅛ cup plus 1 teaspoon (40g) flower paste

Premade white hammerhead stamens, small and micro tips

Hamilworth floral tape (green and brown)

Liquid gel colors (pink, claret, and ivory)

Petal dusts (primrose, lemon yellow, poppy red, burgundy, champagne, pink candy, dusky pink, baby pink, lavender drop, chocolate, brown, leaf green, vine, gooseberry, and olive)

Sugartex Granular Food Color ("Pollen")

Primrose petal cutter, small (1-inch)

PME foam pad with holes (Mexican foam pad)

Veining tool

PME cutting wheel

Rose leaf cutter, small (1¼-inch)

Rose silicone leaf veiner, medium (2½-inch)

MAKE THE FLOWER PASTE BALLS

To make about twelve blossoms for one branch, use 1 teaspoon (10g) of the flower paste to create the mother ball according to instructions on page 192 using pink and claret liquid gel colors and a pinch of the magic black ball (see page 196) for a muted vintage look. Using 1½ teaspoons (15g) of paste each, create only two additional balls, one white and one ivory, to marble with the mother ball. You don't need to create a lighter-colored version of the mother ball.

CREATE THE CENTERS

Cut a 26-gauge wire into three equal-size pieces, one for each blossom. Bundle a combination of five small and micro stamens together in unequal lengths. Fold them in half. Using a piece of half-width green floral tape, secure them to a wire ¼ inch from the top. *(1)* Using needle-nose pliers, bend an open hook in the top of the wire to serve as an anchor for the flower. *(2)* Using a dry brush, apply yellow petal dust and "Pollen" granular color to the anthers. *(3)* Repeat, creating one bundle of stamens for each cherry blossom you plan to make.

Continued

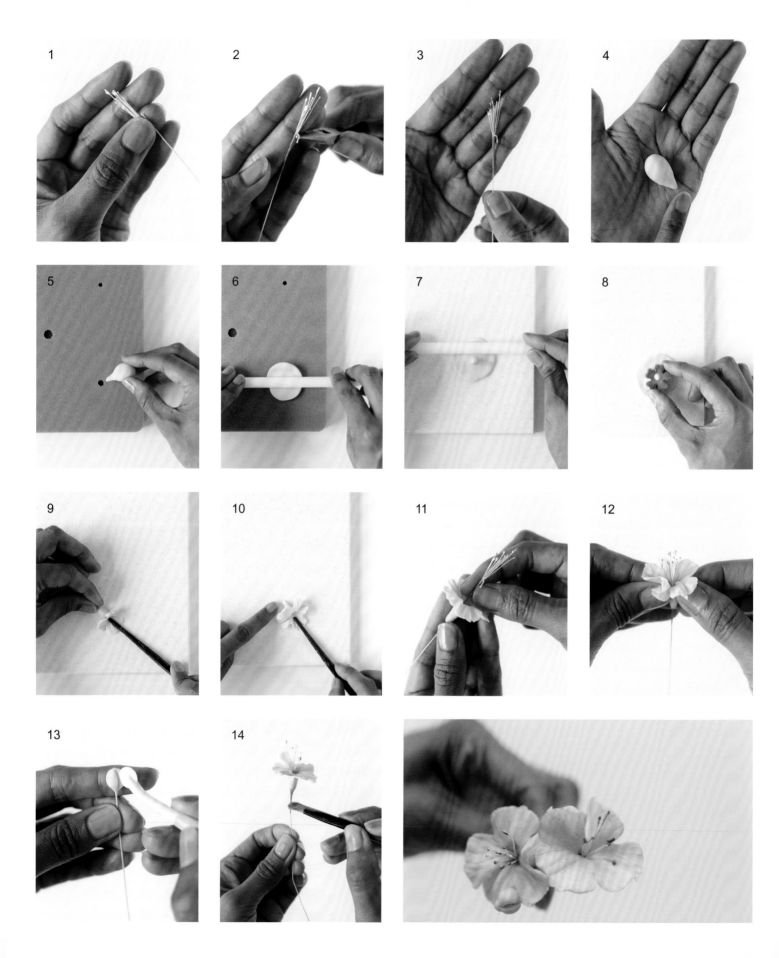

CUT THE BLOSSOMS

Knead a small piece (about 1 teaspoon/10g) of pink flower paste until it is malleable, adding a touch of shortening if the paste feels dry. In the palm of your hand, pinch off and roll a small piece of paste (about 5g) into a teardrop shape. *(4)* Push the pointed end into the second-largest hole of a foam pad with holes. *(5)* Flatten the paste onto the pad with your finger. Using a CelPin, roll back and forth over the paste to widen it before gently lifting it from the hole. *(6)* The shape should resemble a sombrero. Place the flat end onto the smooth surface of a groove board and roll the CelPin from the stalk to the outside edge to flatten the paste slightly. *(7)* Position the primrose cutter with the stalk in the center and cut out a blossom. *(8)* Peel away excess paste and wrap it in plastic wrap for reuse. If it is difficult to release the flower paste from the cutter, use the point of your veining tool to assist.

SHAPE THE BLOSSOM

Gently peel the blossom from the board and rest it on its side on the smooth surface of a groove board. Dip a veining tool in cornstarch and position the point in the center of the blossom. Roll it from the middle to the side of one petal with considerable pressure. *(9)* Repeat on the other side of the petal to create texture, thin the petal, and curl the edges. *(10)* Repeat this step with the remaining petals. Using a ball tool, frill the edges of the petals on a flower foam pad, if desired.

ASSEMBLE THE BLOSSOM

Using a brush, apply a small amount of egg white to the wire hook and wipe away any excess. Hold the blossom at its base and push the end of the wire through the center until the stamens rest in the middle and the hook is anchored in the paste. *(11)* Dip your fingertips into the cornstarch and give the flower stalk a gentle pinch underneath the petals. *(12)* To remove any excess paste, pinch the bottom of the stalk while simultaneously twisting the wire. Insert the wire into the Styrofoam block and set it aside to dry completely, 2 to 4 hours. Repeat steps 4 to 12 to create your desired number of blossoms,

blending the pink color paste with the uncolored (white) and the ivory balls to create variation. For a natural and playful appearance, dry some blossoms standing upright and others with their heads bending down or to the side.

CREATE A BUD

Cut a piece of 26-gauge wire into four equal-size pieces, and using needle-nose pliers, create a closed hook (see peony instructions, page 201, steps 1 and 2). Roll a small piece of pink paste (about 5g) in the palm of your hand to form a teardrop. Insert the hook into the tapered tip of the teardrop and pinch closed the bottom to make a smooth transition with the wire. Using a cutting wheel, create a groove running the length of the bud. *(13)* Insert the wire into the Styrofoam block and set it aside to dry completely, 8 to 12 hours. Repeat if desired to create additional buds.

COLOR THE BLOSSOMS

Use a small piece of half-width floral tape to create a transition from the bottom of the flower stalk, extending partially down the wire. Using a dry brush, apply a mix of pink petal dusts to the petals and bud. Moving in an upward motion, apply a few strokes of dark green and/or brown petal dust over the flower tape to give the illusion of a calyx. *(14)*

ASSEMBLE A BRANCH OF CHERRY BLOSSOMS

To create a stem, stretch and wrap brown whole-width floral tape the full length of an 18-gauge floral wire. Using additional tape, secure a small cluster of blossoms to the top of the stem. Repeat with additional blossoms, trailing them in alternate positions down the stem with a few small leaves (see "Create the Leaves," page 210), if desired. Using a dry brush, apply green and brown petal dust to the branch. For a nuanced finish, curl the stamens of the blossoms with the end of a brush.

CHAPTER TEN

Celebration Cake

No celebration is complete without something sweet, and I can't think of any food that enhances a festive mood more than cake. Made with love and care, this treat transforms any meeting into a truly special gathering that bonds attendees in an experience of joy and sensory gratification. Although using fresh flowers can reflect seasonality, the versatility of sugar flowers is endless. Adorning a cake with these unique confections pays tribute to a special occasion with the generous beauty of petals, lush foliage, and sweet flower buds that can last for years to come. Whether garlanded with an abundant display of multiple blooms or with only one meaningful blossom, a cake decorated with sugar flowers is a remarkable offering to a special loved one.

This three-layer Celebration Cake is made from a rich and moist sponge base that is perfect for using in combination with soft and luscious, velvety buttercream. Assembled as a naked cake, this combination is suitable for tea at a casual gathering (see image on page 88). When wrapped in fondant, however, this sponge cake is elevated to the ideal canvas for a lavish display of sugar flowers that are protected from exposure to the moisture of buttercream. Avoid adding sugar flowers directly to a cake frosted with buttercream, as the oil can stain the petals or, worse, dissolve them entirely.

When I make a Celebration Cake with sugar flowers for weddings, birthdays, and anniversaries, guests are often amazed that the flowers are not real. The question that always follows is "Can I eat them?" These fantastical blooms elevate any cake into a form of edible art, with some considerations. The main ingredient in sugar flowers is of course sugar, but the wires, stamens, and other manufactured parts fused with glue are not meant for consumption.

If guests are reluctant to nibble the petals, the work and love that go into creating these confections make them worthy of saving as a precious keepsake instead. Sugar flowers are fragile once dried and need to be transported gingerly. If you are traveling with sugar flowers to or from an event, stabilizing a Styrofoam block to the bottom of a cardboard box with hot glue provides a foundation to secure the wire of the stem and prevent the flower from tumbling around in the box. Once the flower is secure, generously pad the petals and provide support around the stem with bubble wrap. If possible, hand-carrying the box during transport is preferable, and avoid shipping sugar flowers to avoid breakage. Once taken back home, sugar flowers can be enjoyed for years afterward (see page 197), arranged by themselves or in combination with fresh flowers.

Celebration Cake

This classic Victoria sponge cake recipe is light, airy, and perfect for any celebration. Before decorating it with sugar flowers, the cake layers are assembled with buttercream and sometimes jam or curd, coated with more jam or curd, and then covered in fondant. This step creates an intermediary layer between the cake and the fondant, ensuring they bond in a structurally sound and visually appealing way. To further personalize the cake, use fruit preserves, citrus curd, or even fresh fruit as a delicious surprise.

It is best to bring the cake ingredients to room temperature first to prevent the batter from curdling, and to bake the cake on the same day you assemble it. When whipping up the buttercream, try substituting your favorite liqueur, or even lemon juice, for the vanilla extract, bearing in mind that if you add more liquid, the consistency will change. The final outer layer of fondant creates a smooth canvas for the sugar flowers and protects them from exposure to moisture that would otherwise compromise their keeping quality. Using a premade and store-bought fondant provides a reliable consistency in every climate and makes this final step so much easier to execute. There are many trusted brands available, but I most often use Satin Ice or Massa Ticino (see Resources, page 238). It is important to calculate the size of the fondant layer for each cake, as the layers will vary according to your ingredients, baking climate, and sometimes your altitude.

Fondant acts as a wonderful preservative for the layers, and a covered cake can be kept at a cool room temperature for 2 to 3 days. It is also possible to place the cake in the refrigerator to lengthen its preservation, but storage humidity will cause the fondant to "sweat" when brought to room temperature. If doing so, be sure to remove and store the sugar flowers separately to preserve their integrity. To prevent the cake from drying out, place a piece of plastic wrap against the cut sides.

This recipe is the perfect size to serve eight to ten people; to create a larger cake, multiply the ingredients, keeping in mind the size of your stand mixer and bowl. Always use the best quality and freshest ingredients, including real butter with rich flavor and organic, free-range eggs. Although not necessary, baking belts (see Resources, page 238) will prevent the layers from doming in the middle and relieve you of excess trimmings from leveling the cake. Follow the manufacturer's instructions if using.

Continued

Equipment

Parchment paper

Three (6-inch) cake pans

Nonstick spray

Stand mixer with heatproof bowl, and whisk and paddle attachments

Whisk

Bowls

Large sieve

Spatula

Digital scale

Spoon

Toothpick

3 wire cooling racks

Butter knife

Saucepan

Piping bag fitted with 7/16-inch round cake tip

Two (6-inch) cake boards

Turntable or lazy Susan

Large offset cake spatula or butter knife

Bread knife

Icing edger

Plastic wrap (optional)

Ruler or tape measure

Cornstarch

20-inch nonstick rolling pin

Cake pizza wheel

2 cake smoothers

Cake

1¾ cups (225g) self-rising flour (see Note, page 235)

1½ teaspoons baking powder

¼ teaspoon fine salt

1 split vanilla pod, seeds scraped, or 2 teaspoons vanilla extract or paste

1 tablespoon whole milk

2 sticks plus 2 tablespoons (225g) unsalted butter, at room temperature

4 large eggs, at room temperature

1 cup plus 2 tablespoons (225g) granulated sugar

Swiss Meringue Buttercream

½ cup (120g) egg whites (approximately 4 large eggs)

1 cup (200g) granulated sugar

3½ sticks (400g) unsalted butter, cut into 1-inch cubes and at room temperature

2 teaspoons vanilla extract

Filling

4 to 6 tablespoons fruit preserves or citrus curd (optional)

Fondant

17⅔ ounces (500g) prepared fondant

1 to 2 teaspoons (5g to 10g) vegetable shortening

BAKE THE CAKE

Preheat the oven to 350°F (175°C) and position a rack in the middle.

Cut three parchment paper circles to fit your baking pans and place them in the bottom of your pans. Lightly grease the parchment and sides of the pans with butter or nonstick spray and dust with flour. Set aside.

Rest the bowl of the stand mixer on top of a large piece of parchment paper and fit the paddle attachment on the mixer. To gain as much lightness as possible, hold the sieve high over the bowl and sift the flour into the bowl. Use the parchment paper to funnel any drifted flour back into the bowl. Whisk in the baking powder and salt.

In a separate small bowl, whisk together the vanilla and the milk. Add it to the flour along with the butter and eggs. Mix the batter on low to medium speed to incorporate the ingredients. Stop the mixer and, using a spatula, scrape down the sides of the bowl. Increase the speed to high and beat for 2 minutes, or until the batter changes color from cream to a subtle ivory.

Divide into the three prepared pans, spooning 1½ cups of batter (10½ to 11 ounces /300 to 310g) into each, to ensure each layer bakes evenly. Level the cake batter with a spatula.

Place the pans in the oven and bake for 25 minutes without disturbing. The layers will be done when a toothpick inserted into the center of the cake tests mostly clean with a few clinging crumbs; do not overbake the cakes. Remove from the oven and set aside on wire cooling racks for 2 to 3 minutes. Run a knife around the edge of the cakes and invert each onto a cooling rack. Gently peel off the paper and leave the cakes upside-down for about 45 minutes, or until completely cool.

MAKE THE BUTTERCREAM

Pour 2 to 3 inches of water into a saucepan large enough to cradle a heatproof stand mixer bowl and bring the water to a simmer. Place the egg whites in the heatproof bowl, making sure there are no traces of yolk or grease that would prevent the whites from reaching stiff peaks. Add the sugar and place the bowl over the simmering saucepan, making sure the water never touches the bowl.

To dissolve the sugar and pasteurize the egg whites, use a clean whisk to gently beat and cook the mixture until the crystals have fully dissolved, approximately 2 minutes. Remove the bowl from the water and place on the stand mixer fitted with the whisk attachment. Whisk on high speed for approximately 8 minutes, or until the bowl is cool to the touch and stiff peaks form.

Mix on low to medium speed, adding cubes of butter one at a time. Increase the speed to medium and add the vanilla extract in small drops, until the butter is fully incorporated, and the mixture appears soft and fluffy. Transfer 1½ cups buttercream to the piping bag fitted with the round cake tip and set aside.

APPLY A CRUMB COAT

Place a 6-inch cake board on top of the turntable. Using a large offset spatula, smear about ½ tablespoon buttercream over the middle. Center the first layer of cake onto the board, bottom-side facing down. Using a sharp bread knife, trim the top if necessary to level the cake and brush away any residual crumbs. *(1, 2)* Pipe an even ring of buttercream around the outside rim of the cake to act as a dam for the filling, if using. Fill with 2 to 3 tablespoons of preserves or curd and spread into an even layer. Using your piping bag or a spatula, work from the center to fill the remaining height of the dam with buttercream. *(3, 4)* Smooth the buttercream into an even layer. *(5)*

Continued

Carefully place the second cake layer over top, bottom-side facing down. Check that the cake is level, trimming the top, if necessary. *(6)* Repeat the filling process, finishing with the last layer bottom-side facing up. Check again that the cake is level. *(7)* Using a spatula, add a thin layer of buttercream (known as the crumb coat) around the sides and top of the cake to secure the layers in place. *(8)* Place the cake, uncovered, in the refrigerator to set for 30 minutes.

Take the cake out of the refrigerator and center a second cake board on top. Using the spatula, apply and coat the outside of the cake with buttercream using the two cake boards for guidance. To achieve a smooth finish, run an icing edger or straight ruler along the side while spinning the turntable against the edger. The firmer and smoother the buttercream, the easier it will be to decorate with fondant. Place the uncovered cake into the refrigerator to firm for at least 1 hour. Remove the cake from the refrigerator and carefully remove the top cake board using a sharp knife to assist. Add a layer of buttercream to fill any gaps if necessary and even out the top with a spatula. A cake frosted in buttercream can be covered in plastic wrap and stored in the refrigerator for up to 5 days. *(9)*

COVER THE CAKE WITH FONDANT

Measure the diameter of the cake's top and write it down. Measure the height of the cake and multiply it times two. Add this number to the cake's diameter. This final number is the diameter of the rolled fondant necessary for covering the cake. Lightly sprinkle a clean work surface with cornstarch to prevent the fondant from sticking. Knead 17⅔ ounces (500g) of fondant with a pea-size pinch of vegetable shortening, warming it slightly with your hands. Form it into an even ball. Using a nonstick rolling pin, roll it into a round and even layer about ¼ inch thick and the diameter of your calculation. Gently release the fondant from the work surface and, with your hands, center it over the top of the cake. *(1)*

Use your hands and a cake smoother to gently press the fondant over the top of the cake, eliminating trapped air so that it rests flush against the buttercream. Using one hand to brace the cake and the other hand to pull, stretch the fondant tight against the sides of the cake. Use a cake smoother to finish evening the surface of the fondant. Apply gentle pressure as you glide your tools over the top surface and sides of the cake. *(1)*

With a pizza wheel, trim away the excess fondant from the bottom of the cake. Using a sharp knife, finish the bottom edge of the cake with a neat and clean edge. *(2)* Run the cake smoothers over the top and sides to finish smoothing the fondant. *(3)*

Note: To make enough self-rising flour for this recipe: In a small bowl, whisk together 4 teaspoons of baking powder and ¼ teaspoon fine salt with 1¾ cups (250g) all-purpose flour.

TIPS FOR DECORATING

Use extra branches with leaves or loose wired petals that are still moist as a cushion for your sugar flowers. Moist leaves and petals aren't as fragile and are easier to play around with and arrange. A gentle touch is advised.

As with fresh flower arranging, foliage forms the perfect base for arranging sugar flowers. Or, imagine a forest theme where you decorate a cake with only leaves or use sugar ivy to climb and dance around a cake.

Use focal flowers, such as peonies or roses, for drama and add accents like cherry blossoms for a light finishing touch.

Make sure your cake is cold when decorating with sugar flowers.

Decorating a Celebration Cake with Sugar Flowers

The following example includes versatile decorating techniques that can be adapted to many creative ideas and types of sugar flowers. Although I love using multiple flowers as singles or in clusters like small bouquets, a more restrained aesthetic is just as beautiful. Using leaves or branches at the foot of the cake can make it feel less artificial and mimics the natural posturing of plants. Fresh and organic edible flowers can also replace sugar flower decoration; to avoid wilting or transportation mishaps, place the fresh flowers on the cake shortly before the cake is presented using flower water tubes for the flower stems to maintain freshness. Although it is not necessary, using a turntable will assist in decorating all sides of the cake consistently.

Equipment

½- to ⅝-inch Poly-Dowels
(plastic cake dowels)

Pen or pencil

Scissors

Full-width floral tape

Wire cutters

Needle-nose pliers

Flower picks (flower cake spikes)

Hold the dowel up to the cake and mark it about ¼ inch below the top of the cake. *(1)* Using a pair of scissors, cut the dowel on the mark. Insert it into the cake a few inches from the side or from the middle of the cake to avoid symmetry.

To create small bouquets, use floral tape to bundle blossoms together. Wrap the full length of the clustered stems with tape moving downward from the base of the flowers before wrapping the tape back upward, making sure no wire is exposed. *(2)* Position the taped sugar flowers in front or to the side of the cake to visualize their placement and trim the stems with wire cutters. If lengthening the stems instead, use an additional longer wire, adding tape to secure and cover as needed.

Using needle-nose pliers, insert the taped flowers into the Poly-Dowel. *(3)* If there is room, add extra sugar flowers to the dowel or use an additional or wider diameter Poly-Dowel to insert bigger clusters of sugar flowers. Hold extra sugar flowers next to the cake to visualize their placement before inserting into flower picks and pushing them into the cake. Don't forget to consider the backside of the cake, using extra foliage or flowers to fill any gaps.

Resources

Delftware Pottery

eBay
www.ebay.com

Catawiki
www.catawiki.com

Supplies

Sugar Delites
www.sugardelites.com

Ellen's Creative Cakes
www.ellenscreativecakes.nl

Amazon
www.amazon.com

Bulbs and Peonies

Brent and Becky's Bulbs
www.brentandbeckysbulbs.com

Colorblends
www.colorblends.com

Floret
www.floretflowers.com

Holland Bulb Farms
www.hollandbulbfarms.com

Peony Shop Holland
www.peonyshop.com

Van Engelen
www.vanengelen.com

Flower Arranging Books and Botanical Illustrations

Ariella Chezar with Julie Michaels. *Seasonal Flower Arranging: Fill Your Home with Blooms, Branches, and Foraged Materials All Year Round.* Ten Speed Press, Berkeley, CA, 2019.

Alethea Harampolis and Jill Rizzo. *The Flower Recipe Book.* Artisan Books, New York, 2013.

Maria Sybilla Merian. *Metamorphosis Insectorum Surinamensium.* Lannoo Publishers, Tielt, Belgium, 2016.

Pierre-Joseph Redouté, *The Book of Flowers.* Taschen Books, Cologne, 2021.

Bibliography

Aronson, Robert D. *Below the Glaze: Delftware in Short Stories.* Amsterdam: Aronson Delftware, 2017.

Balai, Leo. *Slave Ship Leusden: A Story of Mutiny, Shipwreck, and Murder.* Sydney, Australia: UTS Publishing, 2014.

Balai, Leo. *Geschiedenis van de Amsterdamse Slavenhandel.* Zutphen, Netherlands: Walburg Pers, 2013.

Dash, Mike. *Tulipomania: The Story of the World's Most Coveted Flower & the Extraordinary Passions It Aroused.* New York: Crown, 2001.

den Heijer, Hank. *Geschiedenis van de WIC.* Zutphen, Netherlands: Walburg Pers, 2013.

Gaastra, Femme S. *Geschiedenis van de VOC.* Zutphen, Netherlands: Walburg Pers, 2009.

Segal, Sam, et al. *The Temptations of Flora: Jan van Huysum, 1682–1749.* Zwolle, Netherlands: Waanders Uitgevers, 2007.

Acknowledgments

A book is never the result of just one person, and I will be forever grateful to all who contributed, supported, and assisted along the way. Thank you to my literary agent, Coleen O'Shea, for your faith in my story, despite my crude draft and clumsy scribbles! I'm fortunate to have you by my side. Thank you, Sarah Owens, for helping express my story. I have been so lucky with a (James Beard) award-winning cookbook author, ceramist, horticulturist, and baker taking me by the hand on this journey. Thank you for walking me home. Thank you, Lisa Regul, my editor at Ten Speed Press, for believing in this book and for your care and guidance. Thank you, Emma Campion, for your masterful and beautiful design, bringing this book to life beyond my wildest dreams.

I wouldn't be anywhere without all the flower vendors I am so lucky to call friends; their offerings of flower gold are a lifeline. Special and a million thanks to Michel de Bruine from Tulip Store EU for sharing your passion and expertise. Your tulips are the most beautiful, always. Thank you, Joshua and Jeremy Scholten from Peony Shop Holland. Thank you, Marlies Weijers and Linda van der Slot from Fam Flower Farm. To all my dear flower friends from Saturday's market, thank you, Joost, Johan, Wilco, and Arjan from J3&W Bloemen; Annemieke and Leonie from Annemieke's Pluktuin; Carla and Rob at City Flowers Ottenhof; and finally, Anja Visser.

Thank you, Adam Lippes, for being such a champion of my work. Sharing your stage so generously has been a highlight in dark times of the pandemic. Thank you, Jill Kargman, Wendy Goodman, and Charlotte Moss, for your friendship and unwavering support. Because of you, a piece of my heart will always be in New York. Thank you, Vanessa Gillespie, for your wisdom and unconditional friendship, and Nathalie Vaandrager, for gifting me flower gold and support so bigheartedly.

Thank you, Laura Derikito, for helping me fly safely. A big thank-you to my Instagram community—the love, loyalty, and encouragement I have received from all of you is a testament of infinite kindness. Thank you, Brian Doben, for including me in your At Work project and capturing me in my happy place.

My deepest thank-you to my husband, Michaël van Heusden, for all your love, support, and boundless patience. This book wouldn't be here without you. My dearest Jan and Nora, seeing you bloom is the most beautiful gift of all. *Ik hou van jullie met heel mijn hart.* This book is for you.

Index

A

Adobe Photoshop, 90
African slaves, 25–26, 30
Age of European Expansion, 17
amaranth, 156, 165
amaryllis, 172
Amsterdam, 18
anemones
    in arrangement, 150
    sugar flower, 212–17
aperture, 96
apple blossoms, 175
Aronson, Robert, 54
arrangement, in photography, 91
auriculas, 140
autumn arrangements
    Floral Renaissance, 162
    The Last Splash, 156–59
    master class, 156–59
    Summer Farewell, 165

B

bleached flowers, 131
Book of Flowers (Merian), 29
bowls, 188
branch and flower stem treatments, 128–29
butter knives, 188

C

Cake, Celebration, 229–37
camellias, 117
cameras, 90, 96
cardboard fruit crates, 188
The Caterpillars' Marvelous Transformation and Strange Floral Food (Merian), 29
Celebrating Abundance arrangement, 146–49
Celebration Cake, 229–37
cellophane tape, 125
Chasing the Sun arrangement, 150
cherry blossom sugar flower, 224–27
chicken wire cushion, 125–26
Chinese bittersweet, 162, 165
Chinese porcelain, 48
chrysanthemums
    about, 161
    in arrangements, 156, 162

clear masking tape, 125
clematis, 140
color wheel, 72
columbines, 140
compost, 131
coneflowers, 150
containers, airtight, 188
contrast, in photography, 92
cornstarch with cornstarch dusting pouch, 186
cosmos, 150, 165
crabapples, 156
cushions, 125–26

D

daffodils
    in arrangement, 143
    conditioning, 129
    removing leaves before arranging, 143
dahlias
    in arrangements, 156, 165
    varieties of, 111
delftware
    about, 47–48
    acquiring, 52–54
    care for, 55
    fabrication methods, 51–52
    for flower arranging, 54
    historic beginnings, 48
    royal influences on, 50–51
    as symbol of affluence, 18
digital cameras, 90
digital gram scale, 188
digital imaging and editing software, 90
digital single-lens reflex camera (DSLR), 90
Dutch East India Company, 18
Dutch Golden Age, 13, 18
Dutch still-life masters, 78–82

E

egg whites, 186
embroidery scissor set, 186
equipment
    flower arranging, 123–26
    photographic, 96
    sugar flower, 184–88
eucalyptus, 172

euphorbia (spurge)
  in arrangement, 162
  hot-water dip for stems, 129

F

falling stars, 165
Fleeting Moments arrangement, 140
floral foam, 126
floral putty, 125
Floral Renaissance arrangement, 162
floral tapes, 187
floral wire, 126, 187
flower arranging
  anchoring plant material, 125–26
  autumn arrangements, 156–65
  as a career, 86
  classic compositional styles, 79
  concept of beauty, 78
  developing a personal style, 84
  embracing irregularities, 75
  equipment for, 123–26
  finding inspiration for, 107
  for the home, 57
  honoring botanical appearance, 72
  honoring flower seasons, 107
  identifying goals and priorities, 77–78
  inspiration from still-life masters, 78–82
  locally sourced blooms, 112–14
  photographing, 94
  satisfaction from, 60
  setting up studio for, 120–23
  sourcing flowers for, 108
  spring arrangements, 136–43
  summer arrangements, 146–53
  for table settings, 60, 63
  timing considerations, 63
  unconventional combinations, 72–75
  using delftware for, 54
  using trimmings and weeds, 117
  winter arrangements, 168–75
flower frog, 125–26
flower paste
  black, uses for, 196
  coloring, 192–94
  creating balls with, 192–94
  recipe for, 190–91
flowers. *See also* flower arranging
  cut, conditioning, 126–28
  extending the life of, 60
  flower market etiquette, 114
  growing calendar, 118, 119
  growing in pots, 118–20
  growing on rooftop terraces, 118–20
  with hollow stems and heavy heads, 129
  inspiration from, 71–72
  local breeders and farmers, 112–14
  making friends through, 117
  seasonal, embracing, 107

sourcing, 108
  spent, recycling, 131
  treating stems and branches, 128–29
  trimming, 117
  from wholesale vendors, 114
flower studio, setting up a, 120–23
FMM Dresden tool (flute and vein tool), 187
foam flower drying tray, 188
foam pad, 187
foliage, creating, 197
footed delftware vessels, 54
frog, 125–26

G

Garden Fantasy arrangement, 175
garden rose sugar flower, 206–11
ginger jars, 54
glass vases, 126
granular color, 188
groove board, 187

H

Hamilworth floral tapes, 187
Hampton Court, 50
hard, woody stems, 129
hellebore
  in arrangement, 172
  conditioning stems, 129
Het Loo Palace, 50
hot-water dip, 129
House of Orange, 50
hydrangeas
  in arrangements, 150, 156, 162
  wilted, remedy for, 129

I

ikebana, 125
Indonesia, 25–26
Indonesian contract workers, 25–26
ISO settings, 96

J

Japanese anemones, 150

K

kenzan, 125
King William of Orange III, 50–51

L

The Last Splash arrangement, 156–59
lazy Susan, 126
leaves, creating, 197
lens, camera, 96
light, in photography, 92
lilacs, 140, 165, 175
lilies, 172

Lippes, Adam, 71
liquid egg whites, 186
liquid gel colors, 188
Love and Light arrangement, 172
lupines, 146

M

malllow, 150
Marrel, Jacob, 27
Mary, Queen, 50–51
memento mori paintings, 79
Merian, Maria Sibylla, 27–31
Merian, Matheus, 27
Metamorphosis arrangement, 136–39
*The Metamorphosis of the Insects
    of Suriname* (Merian), 29, 30
Millet, Jean François, 84
Ming blue-and-white porcelain wares, 48

N

natural light, 92
Nederlands-Indie (Indonesia), 25
needle-nose pliers, 186
negative space, 23
Netherlands
    acquires Suriname, 25
    creative expression in, 17
    cultural diversity, 17
    flower industry, 108
    market flower vendors, 13
    Peace of Breda treaty, 25
    Spanish occupation, 17
    tulip industry, 32–38
New Amsterdam, 25
New York, 25
The Night Watch, 94
9-inch rolling pin, 187
nonstick groove board, 187

O

oak leaves, 156

P

paintbrushes, 188
painter's palette, 188
paper towels, 188
Peace of Breda treaty, 25
peonies
    breeding, 112
    in arrangement, 146
    conditioning, 129
    'Coral Charm', 136
    'Coral Sunset', 136
    growing, 118
    photographing, 97

sugar flower, 198–205
    unfurling process, 136
perfectionism, 99
Peruvian lilies, 172
petal dust
    about, 188
    adding nuance with, 197
petals
    assembling into complete flowers, 197
    creating, 194
phone cameras, 90
photography, 89–99
    arrangementin, 91
    contrast in, 92
    developing your personal style, 99
    documenting your work, 89
    equipment, 96
    flower arrangements, 94
    from hobbyist to professional, 89–90
    light in, 92
    note on perfection, 99
    photographing peonies, 97
    vulnerability in, 99
pin frog, 125–26
plastic wrap, 188
poinsettia stems, hot-water dip for, 129
Pool, Juriaen, 20
poppies
    in arrangement, 146
    hot-water dip for stems, 129
porcelain wares, 48
The Porcelain Jar pottery, 51
pottery factories, 51–52

Q

Queen Mary Stuart II, 50–51

R

ranunculus, 143, 175
raw image file (RAW), 90
Reawakening arrangement, 143
rejuvenator spirit (ethanol), 188
Rembrandt, 94
resealable bags, 188
Rijksmuseum, 17
rolling pins, 187
Romance arrangement, 168–71
rooftop terraces, 118
roses
    in autumn arrangements, 162, 165
    conditioning stems, 129
    garden rose sugar flower, 206–11
    in spring arrangements, 136, 140
    in summer arrangements, 146, 150
    in winter arrangements, 168, 172, 175
Ruysch, Frederik, 20
Ruysch, Rachel, 20–23